Dear Maryann

may your
beautiful
heart blossom
with compassion!
May your
bright spirit
shine!

Love & Blessings,

More Praise for Gail Straub and
The Rhythm of Compassion

"Gail Straub is a warm companion as well as an astute guide in this wise book."

— GEORGE LAKEY, author of *Powerful Peacemaking*

"This is a book of great authenticity, practicality, and heart."

— SHARON SALZBERG, author of
Lovingkindness: The Revolutionary Art of Happiness

"This book goes to the heart of compassion in action. It is a wonderfully wise guide on engaged spirituality."

—JOAN HALIFAX ROSHI, author of *The Fruitful Darkness*

"How many of us have turned away from the ever-present suffering in our troubled world, out of despair and hopelessness about knowing how to help? Gail Straub tackles this issue head-on in this beautiful, wise, and practical book. In showing how our personal well-being is inescapably intertwined with the fate of all beings and the planet as a whole, Gail speaks with a voice of total authenticity, great compassion, and a seasoned understanding of all the challenges, joys, and dangers that one is likely to encounter along the path of service. This book is a guide that can change your life and expand your vision of what you are here for."

—JOHN WELWOOD, author of *Love and Awakening*,
Journey of the Heart

please turn the page for more praise . . .

"Gail Straub's *The Rhythm of Compassion* is an invaluable book for people engaged in some form of social helping—whether it be as teacher or social worker, social change activist or healer. Straub provides tools and insights that will be invaluable for helping us sustain a long term commitment to the transformation of the world. If you don't have a spiritual practice that already sustains you, or if the very idea of "spiritual practice" brings up images of political reaction or inwardness unconnected to serving others, read this book and you'll find a path that can provide balance in your life."

—RABBI MICHAEL LERNER, editor of *Tikkun* magazine and author of *The Politics of Meaning: Restoring Hope and Possibility in an Age of Cynicism*

"Deep as the ocean, penetrating as the wind, purifying as fire, practical as earth, Gail Straub's book is a gift of spirit. A simple and thorough guide to digging back through the layers of life, it helps deliver the reader to the deep well of compassion that dwells within every human heart. What is found within can then be given back to the larger circle of life as love and service."

—JOAN BORYSENKO, author of *7 Paths to God: The Ways of the Mystic*

The Rhythm
of Compassion

The Rhythm
of Compassion

CARING

FOR SELF,

CONNECTING

WITH

SOCIETY

GAIL STRAUB

TUTTLE PUBLISHING
BOSTON • RUTLAND, VERMONT • TOKYO

First published in 2000 by Tuttle Publishing, an imprint of Periplus Editions (HK) Ltd, and Journey Editions with editorial offices at 153 Milk Street, Boston, Massachusetts 02109.

Library of Congress Cataloging-in-Publication Data in Process

ISBN: 1-885203-83-7

Distributed by

USA
Tuttle Publishing
Distribution Center
Airport Industrial Park
364 Innovation Drive
North Clarendon, VT 05759-9436
Tel: (802) 773-8930
Tel: (800) 526-2778

Canada
Raincoast Books
8680 Cambie Street
Vancouver, British Columbia
V6P 6M9
Tel: (604) 323-7100
Fax: (604) 323-2600

Japan
Tuttle Publishing
RK Building, 2nd Floor
2-13-10 Shimo-Meguro, Meguro-Ku
Tokyo 153 0064
Tel: (03) 5437-0171
Fax: (03) 5437-0755

Southeast Asia
Berkeley Books Pte Ltd
5 Little Road #08-01
Singapore 536983
Tel: (65) 280-1330
Fax: (65) 280-6290

First edition

06 05 04 03 02 01 00   10 9 8 7 6 5 4 3 2 1

Design by Dutton & Sherman

Printed in United States of America

Dedicated to my parents, Jim and Jackie Straub, for instilling both a seeker's spirit and social conscience in me.

CONTENTS

PART TWO

THE OUT-BREATH:
CARING FOR THE WORLD

PART THREE

CIRCLING HOME:
WHEN INNER AND OUTER UNITE AS ONE

PREFACE

As far back as I can remember I've been searching for my tribe—those people who feel equally passionate about the care of their souls as they do about the care of the world. I've been blessed to find many of them, including my husband. Along the way I've dedicated much of my life's work to teaching people about the rich and complex intersection between the inner life and the life of service. I've come to think of this relationship between soul and society much like following the in-breath and the out-breath, as in meditation practice. There's a natural time for the in-breath of caring for self and family, and a natural time for the out-breath of caring for the needs of the world. The challenge is to become skillful in following our rhythm—knowing when it's time to go inward and when to go out into the community.

My personal story clearly reflects this quest to balance my inward search with my commitment to society. From early childhood my mother inspired my spiritual search and my father instilled me with a social conscience. As a teenager I was equally inspired to attend religious conferences and tutor inner-city children. During the 1960s I had a growing interest in Buddhist meditation and was involved in nonviolent resistance against the Vietnam War. In the 1970s I joined the Peace Corps eager to explore the diversity of the human condition. My years in Africa combined much personal growth with social contribution. On my return, the Women's Movement deepened my dedication to both inner work and community organizing. My husband, David, and I recognized each other as soul mates through our passion to integrate our spiritual and worldly efforts. In 1981, we created our business, Empowerment Training Programs, to teach people both self-actualization and social conscience. It seems my whole life I've been learning to balance the inner and the outer.

And it seems that so many people are yearning for this balance. As we enter a new century people are taking a long, hard look at the state of their souls as well as the state of the world. In hundreds of letters and personal encounters, students have asked me for guidance in facing their own challenges and the pain of the world. They long for a sense of moral purpose and a way to "give back" to society. They aren't asking for easy answers, nor are they afraid to walk into the heart of human and ecological suffering. My students come from all walks of life and span several generations, ranging from twenty to seventy years old. Some are seasoned activists experiencing burnout and compassion fatigue, and they need the in-breath of personal reflection. Others have done years of self-awareness work and yet feel empty and disconnected, and they need the out-breath—finding their place within the larger social fabric. What they all have in common, however, is their spiritual hunger and a recognition that their own health is inseparable from the health of the world.

As more and more people make this vital connection, they begin the delicate act of juggling soul and society. This book is written to help you balance these two worlds, offering a seamless set of values that unites the inner and the outer. You will learn how to integrate your rhythm so that your inner-care self helps you serve the world, and your caring for the world contributes to your soul. Some of you will find you've been working too hard out in the world, and it's time to move inward, caring for your interior. Others who have worked on your inner life may discover you need to move out and engage with suffering beyond yourself. We will examine themes important to everyone: how to deal with guilt, shame, overwhelm, and burnout. How to answer the important and ever-present questions: Am I doing enough? How do I find the time for more commitments? We will describe the qualities of mature compassion, which diffuse these anxieties and allow us to balance our own needs with the needs of the planet. At the heart of this inquiry is a move away from moral obligation, toward a joyful and spontaneous generosity—the deepest place from which to live and serve.

The process of balancing inner and outer is highly individual and changes with the different cycles of life. In our twenties we are brimming with idealism and long to channel our moral passion out into the world. Later, for some, come the children and a frantic attempt to work a full-time job and meet the needs of a family. As the children grow older we find there are many ways of serving as a family—in a nursing home, a soup kitchen, or planting trees in the community. When the kids have left home and we have climbed the career ladder, we decide to mentor. At midlife and at retirement people from all walks of life are discovering a yearning to give back to their communities.

This book will help you find your own rhythm of compassion caring for yourself and the planet. It is structured by two overarching stories—the personal and the social/ecological. Within these two sagas there are many small stories—my story, my students and colleagues' stories—that tell how we've balanced our own needs while contributing to the world. This book is also an invitation to actively tell your own story and to see how intimately connected it is to the larger tales of the human family and the earth. We live and breathe and learn through stories. The stories in this book don't prescribe how you should be; rather they offer poignant glimpses of life that you can reflect upon and add to your own unfolding saga as you choose.

To bring continuity to the two overarching stories we'll use the metaphor of an archaeological dig. You will unearth the symbolic artifacts that help you tell your own story and connect to the story of society and Earth. In Part One, The In-Breath: Caring for Self, you will excavate your life story as a means to self-understanding and self-care. As you uncover the joy and suffering in your personal story you'll see how it parallels the beauty and heartbreak of the world. In Part Two, The Out-Breath: Caring for the World, you'll unearth the qualities of mature compassion that allow you to respond skillfully to the complex challenges and pain of the world while maintaining your own well-being. We'll see clearly that the insight from your own story is crucial for engaging with the larger story of the human family and the earth.

Each section contains exercises, many of which are designed as ongoing practices that you can incorporate into your daily life. A few thoughts on how best to use the exercises in this book. It's helpful to have a journal and drawing materials as you may discover both words and images as you answer the questions. If you find that gentle, relaxing music helps you quiet your mind and work more deeply please select your preferred music for each exercise. Because many of the exercises are part of ongoing practices often you will return to them more than once. Your answers will change and deepen over time. If you are working with a therapist or support group these exercises can enrich and complement those endeavors. Integrating the practices from these exercises into your life is ultimately what will allow you to sustain your rhythm of compassion, the natural cadence within you that balances inner and outer.

Today we face an unprecedented challenge as we tend to our own spiritual health as well as the soul of a troubled world. We are pioneers in what the Dalai Lama calls "universal responsibility," learning compassion for self and society and Earth. The chapters ahead will demonstrate that both our well-being and the well-being of the planet depend on how skillfully we balance caring for our souls and caring for the world.

Without the in-breath of self-care and reflection we can't sustain our involvement with the suffering of the world, nor do we have the clarity of heart and mind required for the complex challenges we face. On the other hand, without the out-breath of compassionate engagement with society our inner work implodes upon itself leading to the dead end of narcissism and spiritual emptiness. To sustain life on all levels we need to breathe in, and we need to breathe out.

This book acknowledges that we live in a broken world and that we're longing for a way to express our highest values. It is a book about the ethics of caring, an ethic that recognizes that the health of the human psyche and the health of the world are inextricably related. It is my deeply held conviction that we cannot truly heal one of these without healing the other. My greatest hope is that in responding with compassion to the brokenness in ourselves and in all living beings, including the earth, we will become whole again. Such big-hearted caring is our greatest challenge. Perhaps it is also our deepest fulfillment.

PART I

The In-Breath: Caring for Self

Story telling is at the heart of life. . . . In finding our own story, we assemble all the parts of ourselves. What ever kind of mess we have made of it, we can somehow see the totality of who we are and recognize how our blunderings are related. We can own what we did and value who we are, not because of the outcome, but because of the soul story that propelled us. That story is our individual myth.

—*Marion Woodman, from* Leaving My Father's House

INTRODUCTION

The central premise of this book is that our own health—physical, emotional, and spiritual—is inseparable from the health of the planet, and that we can't truly heal one without healing the other. That said, why start with our life stories? Because to tell our stories truthfully is one of the most valuable paths to self-understanding and wholeness. From ancestral times when people sat around a fire to modern times sitting with a therapist, we humans have gained self-awareness through penetrating the joy and suffering in our stories. This awareness has allowed us, in turn, to find compassion for ourselves—to accept our dark unconscious parts and to fully bring to light our gifts.

As a teacher I am privileged to listen to many stories. This is an astonishing process that always startles me with its newness. When a life story is deeply heard, listener and teller are transformed. The teller feels seen and witnessed, somehow purified and more integrated. The listeners see themselves in parts of the saga and suddenly they are not alone and feel more courage.

When I work with students, the first thing we do is explore their life stories, discovering what shaped who they are and what matters to them. Later in our inquiry they begin to connect their personal sagas to the larger world. In this second phase we see a stunning synergy. As they heal their personal suffering they are inspired to reach out and help others. As they encounter society's suffering and work to eliminate it, their personal healing is accelerated. As they repair their alienation from the natural world, aspiring to live more simply and sustainably, they feel less alienation within their own souls. They begin to understand that the inner and the outer are part of the same great circle of life.

Thus we begin our inquiry with the in-breath of self-understanding as the most skillful preparation for the out-breath of caring for the world.

Each of our stories is both utterly unique in its details and universal in the way it touches on larger human themes. It is this intersection—just between the in-breath and the out-breath–that I find most compelling. Here, within this mysterious intersection, we find our healing and our spiritual wholeness. Jesus taught, "Love thy neighbor, as thyself," and indeed it is a lot easier to care for my neighbor if I have real compassion for myself.

The metaphor of a dig is especially appropriate for this book because it helps place our personal stories in the context of a larger narrative. When we dig for a bowl, a tool, or an article of clothing at an archaeological site these individual artifacts fit into the context of a whole society. We too will see how our "soul artifacts" are connected to the larger story of the human family and the earth.

As we dig we don't know exactly what we'll find—some things may shock and sadden us, others may bring healing and joy. And as in archaeology, digging for a story is a many-layered intuitive process more than a linear one. Over the course of time we find fragments of our childhood. Then one day we discover a particular piece of our youth, and as we place it with the other fragments they all come together in a whole and we see something true about ourselves.

In Part One, we will focus on four major areas of excavation:

1. *uncovering a central image* that provides you with a blueprint to heal a core wound
2. *digging for the artifacts from your parents* as a path to understanding your strengths and vulnerabilities
3. *exposing where you belong and where you hide* as a way to connect with the larger human family
4. *unearthing heartbreaks and wake-up calls* as a way to connect with the universal suffering of the world.

These four areas have proven extremely fertile in my own dig and in my work with students. Throughout Part One you will meet some of these students. You will read about Sonya, whose core wound involved having needs and opinions that were not taken seriously when she was growing up. This wound inspired her to create a visionary model of early childhood education in the inner city of Washington, D.C., where the children's ideas are honored and respected. As a young boy, Gary had a mystical experience in the natural world. This gave him a sense of the interconnection of all beings. Today this influences the way he practices medicine, viewing our own health as integral to the well-being of the earth. When Ann's beloved cat, Dutchess, died, she used this experience to reach out to others, and her work as a passionate animal rights advocate began. A workaholic, Dwight finally woke up to the violence of his incessantly busy life. He was able to see how he used it to deaden his deepest feelings and avoid suffering. As he began to heal himself, he was able to be with his dying mother in a tender and heartfelt way.

You will also meet Diane, visionary director of an agency working with the AIDS epidemic. She is searching for ways to sustain her hope in the face of overwhelming suffering. As she deepens her spiritual practice, she learns how to balance activism and acceptance. Finally, there is Pat who retired from a successful military career and was startled to find herself full of rage and violence. Her healing came as she took leadership in the Maine State Prison Alternatives to Violence Program, and her volunteer work in prisons opened the door to her own soul.

I have also included my own story here. I believe that the most authentic way to teach is through the example of my own journey with all its joys and sorrows. In this section you will see how my own healing grew out of heartbreak and wake-up calls, and how I struggle to balance my inner life with my calling to serve the world.

There are parts of my own story I would rather leave out, pretending that they never happened. I like to blow up the good parts, giving them more space than the hard parts. Most of us engage in this little charade of exaggerating certain parts of our life story and leaving out some of the messy parts. To tell our story just the way it is takes a lot of courage. As the gifted *cantadora* Clarissa Pinkola Estes says, "There must be a little spilled blood in every story if it is to carry medicine." But the most difficult parts of our story are frequently the greatest teachers. These difficult places are often where we feel most alive and most in touch with the beautiful mess of the human condition.

My therapist friends tell me that the heart of their work is to listen deeply and awaken the potent story that is slumbering within every person. They tell me that healing the soul begins with a commitment to telling the truth. If we tell our story just the way it is, without exaggeration or understatement, we discover who we are and what matters to us.

It is important to have appropriate expectations before you embark. If you consciously read the chapters ahead and carefully do the exercises, you will be rewarded with greater self-understanding. The artifacts from your story will undoubtedly provide rich insights that you may wish to bring to a therapist, mentor, or support group for further integration. For those of you who have already done much investigation into your story, I encourage you to go deeper still, concentrating on how your story connects you to serving the world.

You will probably not completely figure out your story and what it means to you. That is a life-long endeavor. I ask you also to humbly acknowledge that some parts of your story may not be ready to be discovered. Toward the end of this section you will meet my friend, Maud, who was still digging, turning over, and uncovering her story until she died at age ninety-six. If we're lucky, as long as we're alive we'll be soul digging.

As you dig for your own life story, I hope you will feel my footsteps alongside you.

Exercise: Telling the Truth

First, a reminder about how to best use the exercises in this book. It's helpful to have a journal and drawing materials for the exercises as you may discover words and images as you answer the questions. If you find that gentle relaxing music helps you quiet your mind and work more deeply please select your preferred music for each exercise. There's no need to labor for your answers, simply allow your responses to come naturally and intuitively. Because many of the exercises are part of an ongoing exploration you may return to them more than once. Your answers will change and deepen over time. If you are working with a therapist or support group these exercises can enrich and complement those endeavors.

Close your eyes, quiet your mind, and gently follow your breath until you begin to relax.

Imagine yourself as a spiritual archaeologist going on a soul dig. You are in search of your life story, and your most important tool is your commitment to the truth. Now place your hands near your heart and focus on these words from Kabir's poem "The Time Before Death." Allow the words to open your heart and inspire you to uncover the truth about your story. To tell your story just the way it is, without exaggeration or understatement.

> Friend, hope for the truth while you are alive.
> Jump into experience while you are alive!
> Think . . . and think . . . while you are alive.
> What you call "salvation" belongs to the time
>   before death.
>
> If you don't break your ropes while you're alive,
> do you think
> ghosts will do it after?
>
> —*Kabir*

How do you feel as you contemplate these words? Do you sense any visual images? As you begin your soul dig are you aware of parts of your story that you would rather ignore?

Are there other parts that you tend to exaggerate—either positive or negative?

Now once again open your heart and hear these words from Marion Woodman as if she were talking to you and giving you the courage you need to tell your story as fully as possible:

Story telling is at the heart of life. . . . In finding our own story, we assemble all the parts of ourselves. Whatever kind of mess we have made of it, we can somehow see the totality of who we are and recognize how our blunderings are related. We can own what we did and value who we are, not because of the outcome, but because of the soul story that propelled us.

Take a few moments to reflect on her words. Now make a sacred agreement with yourself to dig for your story as truthfully and courageously as possible. Remember some parts of your story may not be ready to be discovered, and the process of uncovering our soul artifacts is a life-long adventure. If you wish you can write down your sacred agreement.

When you have finished this exercise take some time to read it over. You may want to spend more time writing in your journal or quietly reflecting on your answers.

One

DIGGING FOR A
CENTRAL IMAGE

This image is the one factor in your life that is responsible for every unhappiness. No one else is responsible for it, only you yourself. True, you did not know any better but you do now. Therefore, you are now equipped to eliminate the source of your unhappiness. And please, do not say, "How can I be responsible for other people acting in certain ways again and again towards me?" As I said before, it is your image that draws these happenings to you, as inevitably as night must follow day on this earth plane. It is like a magnet, like a chemical law, like the law of gravity.

—The Pathwork Guide

The "Pathwork Lectures," from which I quote above, have been my central spiritual text for many years.[†] Part of the lectures' brilliance is their demand that we take full responsibility for our stories, most especially the parts that are causing pain

---

† From 1957 until her death in 1979, a gifted woman by the name of Eva Pierrakos gave 258 "Pathwork Lectures," offering a stunning partnership of depth psychology and spiritual law. Like any profound spiritual text the "Pathwork Lectures" have been essential in helping me understand my story.

or unhappiness. Primary among many gifts the lectures have given me is the idea that a certain life experience provides a central image to each of our stories. From this central image we draw a false conclusion about life that then causes a repeated pattern of unhappiness. This image haunts us, coming back over and over as a theme in our lives. It's as if a preview of our journey was stored in this single experience. Often this event is key to understanding the spiritual challenge or wound in our story. For the purpose of our soul dig I have simplified the process of finding the central image, at the same time using many key ideas from the "Pathwork Lectures."

Uncovering this central image is a potent way to begin a soul dig because it requires tremendous self-honesty and cuts through many superficial layers of a life story. Meister Eckhart, the thirteenth-century Christian mystic, said this about cutting through the layers: "A man has many skins in himself, covering the depths of his heart. Man knows so many things; he does not know himself. Why, thirty or forty skins or hides, just like an ox's or a bear's so thick and hard, cover the soul. Go into your own ground and learn to know yourself there." Uncovering the central image goes to the ground of our story. It leads us to a core wound that we need to heal. Finding this wound, then having the courage to face it and transform it, is at the center of all heroic tales including our own.

To uncover an image we search for an unhappy or unfulfilled area of our life . In particular we are digging for an area where we simply cannot overcome a problem even though we genuinely want to. Though we're doing our best to change the problem, it continues to repeat itself again and again. This causes tremendous pain. For some of us the area of suffering is obvious, and for others it's subtle as we hide our pain through masterfully constructed defenses.

Often our earliest significant painful memory can provide the sought after central image. This memory occurs at different times for each of us, but usually it's somewhere in infancy or early childhood. For some of us the earliest painful memory is around the circumstances of our birth. My own story is a good example of how a birth memory can represent the central image, the wound that I need to heal in my life.

My first significant painful memory was that I couldn't drink my mother's milk. It made me sick and I threw up constantly. I was allergic to the very nourishment that would keep me alive. I was fed formula and cow's milk to no avail. As my father later told me, things were getting pretty scary and they worried they might lose me. Finally, I was given goat's milk and at some level I decided to incarnate.

The central image of the allergy to my mother's milk imprinted me with the notion that I was allergic to the nourishment that sustains and strengthens life. From this image I made this false conclusion: I am allergic to nourishment. In the extreme, I concluded that if I were nourished I would die. It's important to note that our false conclusion is usually irrational and causes shame when we finally admit it.

In one way or another, this theme would recur for the next forty years. As I review the repeated places of unfulfillment in my life story I see that I was often unable to be nurtured by my own experiences. I never felt that I was enough. In fact, I was allergic to the nourishment one receives from simply being in the world. I was an overachiever in school, and later, in my work, as I committed to teaching, cross-cultural work, world peace, and empowering women. Yet I refused the satisfaction that came with these accomplishments. I felt I had to do more, and the more I did, the hungrier I felt.

From the moment of birth I also rejected the gentler female qualities that were offered to me by my mother. For much of my life I betrayed my own feminine nature, turning away from my intuitive wisdom, and giving allegiance to the masculine realm of reason and achievement. I could not *be*, so I had to *do*. This spiritual challenge, signaled so early in my life, has been at the center of my journey. My story asks me to heal this wound; to allow myself to feel the satisfaction of being enough, and to embrace the nourishment of being feminine, to accept my mother's milk long after my birth.

To assist my students in digging for a central image, first I encourage them to carefully investigate where they have strong repeated patterns of unhappiness or lack of fulfillment. Places they are doing their best to change, but the pattern of unhappiness continues to recur. They look in the obvious places—relationships, family, emotions, sexuality, body, work, money, creativity, or spirituality among others. Over time they begin to see a common theme in their unhappiness.

Once they have found the common theme they dig deeper asking what am I afraid of, where am I defended, what pain am I hiding from? Then they're ready to uncover when that pain first appeared in their story.

Once they unearth the first painful memory they ask the key question: from this experience what false conclusion did I make about life? I remind them that the false conclusion is usually absurdly irrational: if I am loved, I'll die; if I show my greatness, I'll disappear; if I take care of myself, everyone will abandon me; if I have abundance, I'll be completely alone; if I am happy, disaster will follow close behind.

These false conclusions drawn from our central image are profound and painful—they are our wounds. Once we expose the image we can break the vicious circle of unhappiness caused by the false conclusion.

Assisting my students, I see how gracefully the clues for personal healing are encoded in their central image. One of my students describes the following memory from her first year: "I was in my crib and I was sure there were dancing monsters, skeletons, evil creatures all around. I couldn't rest. I couldn't sleep, because if I slept, if I rested, I would die. That was my central image and my false conclusion. In order to stay alive I had to remain alert, and awake at all costs." This image followed her through high school where she got mono from lack of rest. She continued in overdrive for many years, priding herself on surviving with only two or three hours of sleep. A gifted teacher and education activist she was putting in twenty-hour days, saving the world—and burning out. The dancing monsters from her crib still haunted her.

In our work together, this student began to understand her refusal to rest. She realized her lifelong pattern of over-drive was hiding a deep fear of death. She worked with a trusted counselor and began to heal her fears and find her way to a more balanced way of life. I also encouraged her to find a spiritual practice where she could be nourished by the in-breath of stillness and silence. She discovered that prayer and retreat time in the natural world were great allies in her healing process.

Many people who are deeply committed to social change end up ignoring their own basic needs. Yet exhaustion and lack of self-compassion limit our effectiveness out in the world. This student's central image provided a key to finding her rhythm of compassion. To continue serving she had to understand that compassion is a living circle, starting with herself and then encompassing her work in society.

Not surprisingly the central image in a story usually reflects a universal, spiritual challenge that many people deal with. Though we often harbor the illusion that we're the only one confronting a particular challenge, we're never alone. My students have worked with these common challenges as central themes in their stories: abandonment, self-esteem, trust, fear of life, fear of death, power, despair, aloneness, emptiness, desire for love, and fear of love. It's strangely comforting to know that we're not alone healing our wound. It's enormously helpful to hold our wound as a spiritual challenge. A spiritual challenge is always at the heart of our hero's journey; it is our key to becoming whole. When we realize we're never alone with our core challenge, and that it is the doorway to our freedom—then we're motivated to take responsibility for our lives, to free ourselves from the tyranny of our image.

The following exercise will help you dig for your central image. It's most helpful to investigate your central image over a period of several months or more. Understanding my own image took many months and I had the help of a spiritual mentor. With my students we soul dig for the central image during the course of a year, gradually gathering more information to clarify the image. Answer the following questions for now, let them percolate while you go on to the next chapters, and then come back to dig again, turning over the questions in a new way. You may find you need some help from a counselor or trusted friend to help you interpret your central image and how your false conclusion plays out as a repeated theme in your life. Most importantly, be gentle with yourself; this is potent and challenging spiritual investigation.

Exercise: Digging for a Central Image

Close your eyes, quiet your mind, and gently follow your breath until you begin to relax.

Review your life, looking for areas in your life where you are chronically unhappy or feel unfulfilled. Look for difficult places you are doing your best to change, but where the pattern of unhappiness continues. The obvious places to dig are relationships, family, emotions, sexuality, body, work, money, creativity, or spirituality among others.

Now begin to look for the common theme or thread running through this pattern. Some typical examples would be: fear of intimacy; lack of self-esteem; fear of rejection or abandonment; mistrusting people, the world, or God; lack of self-responsibility, becoming a victim; a negative, cynical attitude toward life; overcontrol or fear of surrender; fear of success and/or happiness. Try to dig without judgment, but rather as a compassionate witness to your story. Take your time and ask for guidance or help in whatever way is comfortable for you.

Once you have uncovered the common theme, try to find your earliest memory of this painful unhappiness. Holding this memory in your mind, ask the key question: From this experience what false conclusion did I make about life? Remember your false conclusion is usually very irrational. It helps to make a statement like this: If I _____ then_____. For example: if I am loved, I'll die; if I show my greatness, I'll disappear; if I take care of myself, everyone will abandon me; if I have abundance, I'll be completely alone; if I am happy, disaster will follow close behind. Most of us feel embarrassed or ashamed when we first expose the false conclusion from our image. Remember: we all have a wound, we're never alone.

Take your time to journal, draw, and feel the pain of your central image and its false conclusion. This is your wound, part of what makes you human and connects you to the rest of the human family.

Now you have exposed your image and you can work to break the vicious circle of unhappiness caused by its false conclusion. What steps do you need to take to continue your healing? Often we need help in clarifying our image. Would it assist you to work with a therapist, trusted friend, or support group? If you have a spiritual practice—meditation, prayer, or time in nature—it's very helpful to use your practice for guidance and continued self-understanding. Take a moment to consider and reflect on your next step in healing your central image, and then write it down as a commitment to yourself. Remember, to understand and heal your core wound caused by the central image takes time, patience, courage, and support. The power of your image will continue to reveal itself for many years; with increasing self-awareness you will be able to free yourself from its hold at deeper and deeper levels.

Two

UNCOVERING THE ARTIFACTS WE INHERITED FROM OUR PARENTS

The dotted line my father's ashplant made
On Sandymount Strand
Is something else the tide won't wash away.
   —*Seamus Heaney, from "The Strand"*

For better or worse, our parents are often the most important people in our story. Some of us were blessed with parents who gave us love and nourishment. Others had parents who caused unspeakable suffering. Some of us know our parents well, others have never met, or barely know them. Some of us are proud to resemble our mothers or fathers, and others say they have nothing in common, or worse, they pray never to end up like their parents.

As we continue our soul dig we discover how our parents shaped who we are. We have already seen the role my mother played in the central image in my story. So often our mothers or fathers have an indelible impact on what matters most to us. And so often the lessons we are compelled to learn from our parents are the very teachings that allow us to go beyond ourselves and reach out to the world. The artifacts from our parents offer us both our strengths and our vulnerabilities. When we can honestly acknowledge both—no matter how much we may have suffered—we enter into a mature relationship with our parents as well as ourselves. The following stories of my parents and Mili's parents offer two contrasting portraits.

My mom, Jacqueline Walsh Straub, came from an Irish Catholic family and was the eldest daughter of nine children. She was the only one of the Walshes who left Colorado for the East Coast and the only one and who married a non-Catholic. Still, it was unquestioned that I would attend Mass every Sunday, regularly go to confession, and receive communion. Sunday Mass made a lasting impression on me but not for the reasons my mother intended. I was not so much captivated by the theology as I was by the sensual and ritual aspects of the service. I loved the incense and candles, the vibrant colors of the priest's garb, the smell of my mother's good Sunday perfume, and the way the host melted in my mouth at the communion rail. I especially remember my mom kneeling in prayer with her black rosary beads. Today I consider the beads one of my most precious possessions and I use them for daily prayer.

My mother's devotion was also filled with suffering. When my sister was born, my mother had her second cesarean birth. The doctor knew if she gave birth again she could lose her life. He proceeded do a tubal ligation, and because of the Vatican's ban on birth control, my mother was excommunicated. She fell into a deep depression and spent many years petitioning to be reinstated as an official member of the Catholic Church. After fifteen years her petition was granted.

To this day I am fascinated by my mother's faith. She didn't leave the church in spite of her unjust censure. One of my greatest regrets is that I never had a chance to talk with her about the source of her beliefs. I was only twenty-three when she died, and my religion at the time was social activism. The farthest thing from my mind was Catholicism and what it may have meant to her. In spite of my mixed feelings about the church, my mother's devotion shaped the very roots of my soul. My mother taught me that faith is central to living, that sometimes suffering comes along with spiritual commitment, and that there are, and will always be, unanswerable questions.

If I remember Jackie Walsh Straub with her rosary beads, I also remember her with her oil paints, charcoal sketches, and watercolors. She chose covered bridges and old country stores as her subjects and took watercolor classes the summers that we spent in Maine. She could also do hilarious caricatures of my high-school classmates. I liked her hands when they were stained with paint and ink. My mom loved color, she loved beauty, and she loved being a woman. It has taken me a long time to appreciate these gifts. After much resistance I finally realized the obvious: she had given me the blueprint for my womanhood. My sensual joie de vivre, my concern for others, the love of my home, and the ritual celebrations I host to bring people together are all tributes to her.

My mother gave me the gift of faith and an appreciation for the beauty of the world. My father asked me to put that passion into action. Jim Straub came from a dirt-poor family. When he was twelve, during the height of the great depression, he tragically lost his father and his only sister. He was raised by my remarkable grandmother Bessie Straub and the Germantown Boys Club. My pop, as we all called him, had faced more human suffering by the time he was an adolescent than I have as a woman of fifty.

Yet my father built a full and meaningful life from the direst circumstances. He became a captain in the Army, then found a position at one of the finest private schools on the East Coast, where he was a gifted teacher loved equally by students and faculty. He gave my brother, sister, and me an exceptional education. My father never had much money, yet he managed to provide us with a rich childhood.

Above all else he was a stoic. He taught me to accept life just as it is, but never be complacent about its injustices. My Pop balanced this paradox of acceptance and responsibility with great aplomb. My spiritual challenge has been to reconcile these opposites—to balance my faith in life, and my passionate desire to fight for ecological and human justice. On certain days when I find this difficult, I can hear my father's words of encouragement.

My father imprinted my social conscience, and he also gave me a love of beauty and craftsmanship. To witness him at work in his shop was to see his very essence. I remember him in his khaki smock, covered with sawdust and smelling of shellac. He was always making a lamp, or a cabinet, or restoring some precious antique. He was a magician and the wood came alive in his hands. Both my parents gave me a deep appreciation of artistry and beauty. My mother was saying to me, bring beauty into your life and nourish your faith. My father was saying to me, bring beauty into the world and sustain your hope.

Only after hearing hundreds of horror stories from participants in my workshops did I realize how blessed I was to have had such loving parents. Perhaps because my husband, David, and I lost our parents before we reached forty years of age, our appreciation of them has been heightened. Of this I am sure, my life is an attempt to blend the qualities my parents gave to me. As I deepen my inner life I am honoring my mother, and as I contribute to the world I pay tribute to my father. The spiritual investigation required to fully understand the potency of our parents' legacy takes patience, courage, and a willingness to forgive. Mili's story is in stark contrast to mine and yet, remarkably, her difficult memories of her parents have also been a source of inspiration and have led her to a life of service.

Mili's Story: A Lesson of Love

Millicent Wright is a gifted social worker who helps families at risk hold on to their children. She came to her life work after digging into her early wounds and ferreting out her family secrets. Her parents brought abandonment, abuse, and rage into her life. But from this, she also learned the power of forgiveness and the strength of abiding love.

"My earliest memories of my father were treacherous," she explained. "We were from Chicago and Al Capone was his hero. My father had a mean side and was alcoholic. He was verbally abusive and as the years went on, he beat the shit out of my step-mom. I went to the hospital with her once after he pushed her down a flight of stairs.

"My biological mother abandoned me and finally committed suicide. When I was a child my father sexually abused me and I couldn't bear to face these memories. When I was eighteen I got pregnant with a boyfriend and gave my son up for adoption. Then I started up with drugs and alcohol. I kept on wondering, What was my life asking of me? How could I survive, much less thrive? I tried to hide my pain by pretending I was fine. But it was my cats that took the brunt of it. I beat one cat, Arbor Ann, many times, just short of breaking her bones. I threw the other, Charlotte Grace, on the floor so hard I was sure I'd broken her leg. All the years of pent-up fury were now exploding on my beloved cats. I felt overwhelming shame and guilt and was sure I was truly evil. Yet, by the grace of God, I found a gifted counselor who guided me through the darkest corners of my psyche.

"When I started therapy I tried to break the endless cycle of abuse. I wrote my father a letter and said if he wasn't going to treat me with respect, I didn't want to talk to him. I never heard back. When I graduated from the University of Michigan, I sent him an invitation to the ceremony. But there was no reply.

"Fifteen years later I found out my father had throat cancer. My first thought was, 'Is this payback, or what?' I didn't want him to suffer, but I had no desire to see him. Finally my stepmother called. He wasn't going to last long. So I packed my bags and drove for two days, sobbing the entire way. When I arrived he didn't recognize me.

'Dad, it's me. It's Mili.'

As he let me in he said, 'I don't want any pity.'

I said, 'I haven't come for pity. I've come to say good-bye.'

"We began to relax looking at his beautiful view of Lake Michigan. Then my father reached for my hands and I knelt down in front of him. 'I came to tell you I'm not angry anymore. I'm sorry it took me so long to work it through.'

He said quietly, 'You had a lot to be angry about.'

"All I wanted was to drink in everything about him. My eyes grew as big as the Empire State Building as I began taking in my father: his mannerisms, his hair, his hands. Dad died several months after this visit. My final memory is of the soft gentle touch of his hands in mine.

"My story is about healing and forgiveness. Today I know that God is truly in my heart. I also believe I must do something with these early memories and use my story to help others."

When I first heard Mili's story, with many more horrendous details than appear here, I felt she had taken me into a veritable inferno, and yet she somehow managed to find her way out. I asked her how she was able not only to survive her story, but also to come out as a wry and loving woman making a significant contribution to many people's lives. With great humility she told me that it was hard work and a lot of grace. She had no illusions; she knew that her story could easily have left her bitter and full of self-pity.

Even in the most difficult circumstances there are life-giving ways to respond to the challenges within our stories. Mili got help from a therapist, she did battle with her demons, she found God, and rather than indulge in her pain she offered the lessons from her immeasurable suffering to help others. The difficulties she endured from her parents gave her the qualities that make her a gifted healer: an uncanny resilience, a rare spiritual wisdom, and a profound empathy for the human condition.

Once we uncover the impact of our parents, one of our most significant challenges is to grow up and emotionally leave home. We gather the positive and negative artifacts, making the most of their lessons as we move out into the world. Some of my students, who are well into midlife, still haven't done this.

It's a turning point in our life journey when we can genuinely say, "This is my mother, this is my father. They did certain things well, and they made lots of mistakes. They were human. I forgive them, and I love them." Mili's story illuminates how this is possible even with the direst situation. This kind of leaving home unties us from our parents, setting us free to create our own lives. And this kind of liberation unleashes enormous energy and creativity for contributing to our families, our communities, and our planet.

Exercise: Uncovering the Artifacts
Your Parents Left You

Close your eyes, quiet your mind, and gently follow your breath until you begin to relax.

Continuing your soul dig, you will search now to uncover the artifacts your parents left you. You are searching for ways, positive and negative, that your parents shaped who you are and what matters most to you. These artifacts from your parents offer you your strengths and your vulnerabilities. When you can honestly acknowledge both—no matter how much you may have suffered—you enter into a mature relationship with your parents as well as yourself.

Place your hands on your heart and focus on the qualities of patience, courage, and a willingness to forgive. These are the tools you need to understand the artifacts from your parents. Journal any words or images that may come.

Envision your mother in front of you and simply allow a free flow of images and words to come to you. Don't judge or censor—just let it flow. Now dig a layer deeper and ask, What feelings do I have when I think of my mother? What are the most important impressions my mother made on me? Again, don't judge or censor negative or positive. From these words, images, feelings, and impressions, ask yourself, What are the most important artifacts—strengths and vulnerabilities—I received from my mother? How have these artifacts shaped who I am and what matters to me? Take your time to journal and reflect.

Now envision your father in front of you and simply allow a free flow of images and words to come to you. Don't judge or censor positive and negative—just let it flow. Now dig a layer deeper and ask, What feelings do I have when I think of my father? What are the most important impressions my father made on me? Again don't judge or censor negative or positive. From these words, images, feelings, and impressions, ask yourself, What are the most important artifacts—strengths and vulnerabilities—I received from my father? How have these artifacts shaped who I am and what matters to me? Take your time to journal and reflect.

To grow up you need to make the most of the artifacts from your parents, and then take the steps to emotionally leave home and move out into the world. Take a moment to gather together the positive and negative artifacts from both your parents. Open your heart and in whatever way feels genuine try saying and feeling these words: "This is my mother, this is my father. They did certain things well, and they made lots of mistakes. They were human. I forgive them, and I love them." These words may be extremely difficult if you had a difficult relationship with your parents. Try saying this over a period of time, like a prayer that you gently grow into. Take time to journal and reflect.

This kind of leaving home unties you from your parents, setting you free to create your own life. It unleashes enormous energy and creativity for you to contribute to your family, your community, and the world. Be gentle with yourself and take one step at a time. If you need help to free yourself from your parents, find a good therapist or support group. Bring your desire for this freedom into your prayers and meditation. Write down your next step in emotionally leaving home, and make a commitment to doing this.

Three

EXCAVATING WHERE YOU BELONG AND WHERE YOU HIDE

There is no house like the house of belonging.
—*David Whyte*

You began by excavating your central image, then the artifacts from your parents, and by now you have some of the major themes for understanding your story. Now you will dig a level deeper to uncover some of the more subtle layers of your life story. You want to expose two opposites—where you belong and where you hide. Our place of belonging is where we feel most known and accepted. It's a source of strength and frequently a guidepost to our life's calling. The place of hiding is where we feel most alienated and where we wear a false mask to cover our true self. Our mask is usually an area of hidden yet intense suffering. It offers a potent way to link with the larger suffering of humanity. Because we often unwittingly swing between these opposites of belonging and hiding, it's a great relief to consciously identify them. Full awareness of both of these forces enriches our self-understanding and our connection to the world.

Where You Belong

To belong is to feel at home with yourself. In a life story, a place of belonging is that place where you feel most alive, most yourself. You feel known and accepted for who you are. For many of us there is a certain area of our childhood where this belonging first occurs. For others the experience of belonging doesn't come until later in life. It can come in a wide diversity of places including books, music, sports, helping others, art, science, politics, travel, nature, or a certain person. Wherever it occurs, our place of belonging has a significant impact on who we are and how we find meaning.

My Story

I was blessed to find a sense of belonging early in my life. Vivid in my memory are the hundreds of hours I spent with my sister, Joanie, exploring the landscape in our backyard. The brook behind our house was called the Pancake Run and we explored her in every season. In the winter we skated on her, as the spring came we picked luscious bouquets of violets and lily of the valley from her banks, in the summer we swam in her cool waters, and in the autumn we followed her every stone down to the Brandywine River. Like monkeys we climbed every tree in the large field across the brook. The Bubble and Squeak Railroad was just beyond the brook. Tramps and hobos, men who had ventured out into the world, lived near the tracks, and we were always on the lookout for them. I recall these hours in nature as glorious and timeless.

My dad helped run a camp in Maine, and the New England summers are also among the idyllic memories of my childhood. It was the happiest time for my family. My father was utterly at home in this rustic environment, and my mother was relaxed. She did more painting during our Maine summers than at any other time in her life. Our tiny summer cabin overlooked the lake, with Mt. Kersage as the sentinel, standing guard. The loons woke us up and put us to sleep. I loved hiking and exploring, canoeing and swimming, and gathering blueberries and flowers. God was everywhere.

The natural world is my soul food, my true church, and my first and oldest love. In nature, I felt completely at home, and yet surrounded by immense mystery. My love of the earth was fierce and passionate. As I entered my early teens I knew I wanted to share this passion with others. I felt an insatiable curiosity about the different cultures on our earth. By the age of seventeen I had launched my role as a citizen diplomat in South America as an American Field Service exchange student. I would eventually travel and work in over twenty different countries. My love affair with Maine and the Pancake Run had opened the door to the world and inspired me to connect with the whole human family.

There is a striking connection between my childhood place of belonging and where I am most at home in life. Because I felt so alive and so myself in nature it became central to both my inner life and my calling in the world. I go to the natural world for spiritual guidance and renewal. My decades of cross-cultural work and ecological activism were born from my early love affair with the earth. For me the natural world is the bridge between my story and the eternal story. Gary offers another example of the powerful role that belonging plays in our story.

Gary's Story: We Are Stardust

Gary Gurka is an allergist and physician practicing in the Boston area. His childhood memory of belonging has played a key role in his commitment to healing both people and the earth.

"As a child," he tells us, "I felt most at home under the stars. When I was eleven, I had my first experience of belonging to a larger world. I often played by myself in the woods and on this particular day, I was naked. I'd painted my body with leaves and clay, then I came upon a heap of charcoal someone had used to make a fire. I painted myself with charcoal dust. What happened next makes no sense to my rational mind, so I would have to call it a mystical experience. The charcoal became stardust—the original stuff that everything came from when the universe was born. In that moment, I became part of something much larger. It was like standing on the rim of the Grand Canyon or seeing the face of your newborn child.

"When I returned to the house, I had a form of temporary blindness. For awhile, everything seemed too bright. An eye doctor found nothing wrong. But for months I couldn't walk down the street without dark glasses, and I often had to wear them inside. Though I could only see dim shapes, I had this strange feeling that I knew where everything was. My experience in the woods had taught me there is much more to reality than what we touch or see.

"As I become more aware of the suffering in my own story, I find I am a better healer and physician. I have learned to balance my gift for rational diagnosis with the clues I pick up in the intuitive realm. One young woman came to me with a recurring bacterial infection. As I listened to her symptoms I got an image of a large foot placed threateningly above her face and chest. I asked, 'Who steps on you all the time?' She began to tell me her story, and to describe her lifelong suffering, and at that point, she began to get better.

"It's compelling to note that the two major causes of death in this country are heart disease and cancer. These two afflictions also wound the earth. A hardened heart, a lack of caring, causes heart attacks. It keeps us from feeling our connection with all other living things. Cancer is about disregarding boundaries. It knows no limits. Like cancer cells, we devour the earth. We subjugate plants, creatures, and the land to our willful needs. No one species should encroach on all the rest. What I learned in the woods, as a child, has helped me to see how all our joys and suffering are connected. I'd like to live the rest of my life, as a doctor and a healer, honoring the fact that we are all part of that original stardust."

As a young boy Gary experienced the inherent unity of all living things. As he became one with the stardust he had a visceral sense of joining the story of the universe. This experience of belonging was not only a great blessing to Gary, it also offered him the keys to his profession and profoundly shaped his calling. Today, Gary is a doctor who balances his gift for rational diagnosis with the wisdom of intuitive knowing and a belief that all things are interconnected.

A friend of mine with a terribly difficult childhood found her only sense of belonging through books. As a young girl she spent long hours in the library surrounded by her beloved books, ideas, and imagination. As she says, books were her survival. Today she's a researcher.

One of my students, while excavating his place of belonging discovered he felt most at home with his grandmother. In particular, he loved how she taught him through her vivid storytelling. This man is a talented therapist who sees his work as listening deeply to his client's stories.

Our early sense of belonging can signal what matters to us. It can provide the love that sustains us or the fire that lights our passion. Sometimes our belonging takes place in a dramatic experience such as Gary's stardust story. For others the feeling of being at home comes in subtle moments in our story and we have to really pay attention to find this artifact. In all cases we are on a quest to find the place where we are most at home on a soul level.

Exercise: Finding Where You Belonged

Close your eyes, quiet your mind, and gently follow your breath until you begin to relax.

Continuing your soul dig now you excavate the childhood place where you most belonged, the site where you felt most known and accepted. Often this is a place or time where you felt most alive. It's a source of strength and frequently a guidepost to your life's calling.

Review your life for the times you felt most at home with yourself, most alive. This feeling can come from almost any area—books, the arts, nature, science, or a certain person. Simply allow a free flow of images and words to come to you.

What are your most vivid memories of belonging? Often these memories have distinct sensual aspects—smells, sights, sounds, tastes, or textures. How has this sense of belonging impacted where you are most at home in life, and how you find meaning? Has your experience of belonging offered keys to your calling in life? At this phase of your life where are you most at home? Take time to reflect, draw, and journal.

What can you do to deepen your sense of belonging, the feeling of being fully alive? Make a commitment to doing at least one thing this week toward that goal.

WHERE YOU HIDE: EXPOSING THE MASK YOU HIDE BEHIND

Truly, it is in the darkness that one finds the light, so when we are in sorrow, then the light is nearest of all to us.

—*Meister Eckhart*

Just as it is important to find our place of belonging, so it is essential to find the site of our alienation. This time, you will dig for the mask you use to hide your true self. Our mask is a facade we use to avoid our pain and suffering.

Exposing the mask in our personal story connects us with two essential aspects of the human story. The first is our primal need to be loved and accepted. The second is our misconception that to be loved we need to hide our humanity, to cover up our vulnerabilities and imperfections. One of the most stunning things I witness as a teacher is the way so very many people try to mask their needs and vulnerabilities. We all think we need to be perfect in order to be loved.

Most of us suffer from our own unique brand of perfectionism. Here are some variations on the theme I've heard over the years: "I have to take care of everyone else perfectly in order to deserve love myself." "If I am not up to my highest standards then I am unworthy of love." "If I stop striving for perfection I will disappear." "I can do everything myself, I don't need any help." "If I am not perfect God will never accept me." "I am always able to be objective and see the best in people and life." "I don't have any needs." The tyranny of perfectionism is deadly. We can't possibly live up to the standards and dictates of our mask. My own story illustrates how our mask of perfectionism creates a vicious circle that traps us in our own game.

My sister was born only fifteen months after I came into the world, and so I formed the belief that to get love, especially my father's love, I needed to distinguish myself by being "the best" at everything I did. Love was equated with doing, performing, and overachieving. I perfected this mask in high school and continued relying on it until my midthirties when I entered rigorous spiritual counseling. On the outside I was successful, hopping around the globe and saving the world, but on the inside there was an emptiness nothing could ever fill. I was blessed to find a gifted counselor who helped me dismantle the mask of perfection I presented to the world.

I was stuck in a vicious circle; achieve more to be loved more, my mask voice said. Doing well wasn't sufficient. I had to be the best. I couldn't show the world that I had needs. I had to be the strong independent woman who keeps doing no matter what. Ironically our masks manifest the exact opposite of what we intend. My mask of perfectionism was supposed to get me love. In fact this tyranny of "being the best" had deeply isolated me from people.

In my late thirties, a key event helped me break my mask of invulnerability. I underwent surgery to remove a large ovarian cyst. I came to understand that the cyst represented my intense overdrive and my constant need to be the best. This masculine overdrive, had literally taken over my ovary, and was attacking the feminine center of my body. I was absolutely terrified of the surgery. I simply couldn't mask that terror because it was so fierce. I had to ask for help, lots of help. Finally, mercifully, I couldn't be the best. I was a person with needs and fears, like all of us I was a beautiful mess. As my mask began to dissolve, I felt a deep sense of acceptance.

As we heal our false mask, we arrive at a place where our personal pain joins us with the pain of the human story. We become aware of one the poignant ironies of the human condition; the false mask we build to get acceptance is often the very thing that isolates us from others, when in fact the vulnerable, needy parts that we deem unacceptable are the very things that connect us and make us real to others. Feeling the painful irony of our mask and understanding how this connects us to the rest of humanity is a crucial step in our spiritual growth.

Unless we see the universality of our pain, we can easily get stuck in endless self-examination. Once we recognize that the suffering in our story links us to the suffering of all living things, our own drama is less consuming. The false mask is not only the tyrant of the soul, it also is the tyrant of our present day society, for it keeps people imprisoned in their own wounds incapable of giving back to the ever unfolding story of life.

A dramatic example of the false mask is exemplified by one of my students who came from an abusive childhood. Alcoholism and violence marked her family history. She says this about her mask: "I tried to hide my pain by putting on a mask of being just fine. I pretended to be incredibly strong, I can do everything, I don't need anybody. I'd seen my mom do it after my dad beat her up. I'd watch her put makeup on to cover her bruises. So, I was all smiles, and 'hi how are you's.'" As long as she denied her pain this woman was unable to heal or live fully. When she began therapy she entered the long, courageous journey of feeling the immensity of her suffering. It took many years to heal, and at times the going was tough. She still has days when the old mask returns and the false self says, "I can do everything and I don't need anybody." But over the years she's cultivated the spiritual tools and the support system she needs to dismantle the mask once again.

Today this person is a gifted counselor who helps people from abusive and violent backgrounds. Her story is particularly moving and instructive. In spite of living through unthinkable suffering, she avoided victimization. She once told me that at a certain point in her therapy she knew with great certainty that all her pain had lead to her calling to help others. By using the lessons from her story to heal others, in some mysterious way her suffering made sense. Her story is a source of great inspiration, a reminder of the power of offering our stories to something larger than ourselves.

A Roman poet spoke about the lacrimae rerum, the tears that are in things. When we have the courage to take off our mask and face our fears and inadequacies, we discover how the very feelings we try to run away from—sadness, loneliness, and fear of being unloved—link us to the heart of the world.

Exercise: Exposing Your Mask

Close your eyes, quiet your mind, and gently follow your breath until you begin to relax.

Now begin to dig for your mask, the place in your story where you cover your true self— where you adopt a facade in order to be loved. Remember your mask often covers your needs and vulnerabilities; it says I need to be perfect in order to be loved.

Allow a visual image of a mask covering your true self to come to you. What does it look like? What do you feel as the mask covers you? Now ask yourself, What is my unique brand of perfectionism? How do I act out the misconception that I need to be perfect in order to be loved? Write down specific examples. Remember, the tyranny of your perfectionism creates a vicious circle in which you have to keep getting "more"perfect. You can't possibly live up to its standards. Take time to reflect, draw, and journal.

Once you have exposed your mask become aware of the poignant irony of your perfectionism. Can you see that the false mask you wear to get acceptance actually isolates you from others? Can you feel the precious energy you waste maintaining this facade? Now imagine yourself taking off your mask. Gradually expose your needs, fears, and vulnerabilities—the beautiful mess of your humanness. Can you feel how this makes you real and connects you to others? Can you feel the creative energy this releases? Take time to reflect, draw, and journal.

It takes time, courage, compassion, and support to uncover your mask. Sometimes we need a counselor or support group. Your chosen spiritual practice is always helpful in keeping you honest about when you've put your false mask back on. Here are some simple questions that can help you stay aware of your mask. Am I covering my needs and vulnerabilities? Am I stuck in my own unique brand of perfectionism? Do I find myself constantly striving to be more and more perfect? Am I acting in a way that betrays my true self in order to get love? The more often you courageously expose your false mask, the less power it has over you. Remember your fear and shame of your mask—feed it and allow it to grow stronger. Above all, be gentle and loving with yourself when you find you are wearing your mask. We all have a mask, and it is part of what connects us in our human condition.

Four

UNEARTHING BROKEN HEARTS, RADICAL SURPRISES, AND WAKE-UP CALLS

When I am sad, I am radiant
When I am broken, content
When I am tranquil and silent as the earth
My cries like thunder tremble heaven

—Rumi

As we gather more and more artifacts our story begins to fill out and mature. Now we can use these insights to help us dig even deeper and uncover some of the most complex parts of our story. Confronting the wound in our central image gives us courage; the artifacts from our parents offer strength; and knowing where we belong and where we hide shows us that we need not mask any part of our humanity. Slowly but surely we are becoming more confident that no matter what happens in our story we can face it, learn from it, and allow it to connect us with the ever unfolding eternal story.

Drawing on this confidence we're ready to unearth the broken heart and the radical surprise in our story—where we are broken and where we are startled awake. The way we relate to our brokenness determines whether our heart awakens or closes, whether we find meaning in our suffering, or are lost in futility and despair. A radical surprise is a vivid wake-up call that shakes us out of our trance, and leaves us changed. Both these artifacts shatter us and cause us to fall apart in a certain way. They remind us how fragile life is, and how precious the gift of our existence is.

BROKEN HEARTS

In nearly every story I have heard there is a broken heart. Sometimes our own heart shatters through violence, abandonment, loss, or tragedy. Sometimes the heart of one dear to us breaks, and we are deeply affected by their sorrow. This brokenness is another of life's initiations and furthers our connection with the human family and the earth. In a mysterious way this very brokenness is our connection to the unbroken whole.

At a young age, my mother suffered from rheumatic fever that left her heart vulnerable to infection. Though she was healthy during my childhood, by the time I was an adolescent she was in and out of hospitals with a strange disease. Her doctors were unable to diagnose it, and we lived with her anxiety. It must have been excruciating for her to not know why she was so sick. My father took over the cooking and domestic duties when my mother was hospitalized. He ran the house with elegance and efficiency. There was never any talk of how afraid we were. The stiff upper lip ruled our house, and we covered our fear with activity.

My mother died at the age of fifty-five after pioneering open-heart surgery. At the time, I was in the Peace Corps in West Africa. I had taken leave to be with her for the surgery and was terrorized, seeing her in the intensive care unit with tubes everywhere, looking like she had died already. But she made it through the next several months. My last memory of my mother was on a summer's day. She was lying on a chaise, admiring her flower garden. "How good it is to be alive," she said, "how wonderful the sun feels."

The morning before the telex arrived at the remote village in West Africa where I was stationed, I got violently ill. I was shaken to the core with gut-wrenching vomiting, and a German doctor could find no cause so he sent me home to rest. Several hours later the headmaster of the school where I was teaching called me. *"Votre mère est mort,"* he said. (Your mother is dead.) My violent illness had occurred at the precise time she expired.

I immediately went into denial and stayed there for fifteen years. I now know from reading Hope Edelman's ground breaking book, *Motherless Daughters,* that a long period of denial is not unusual for women who lose their mothers at an early age. My heart was shattered by this loss. I couldn't bear the pain so I returned to my familiar pattern of achievement, saving the world and ignoring my own pain.

In most stories there are several wounds that come with the broken heart. In my story, the most obvious is the unbearable loss of my mother. Equally important was the fact that I could not express my fear throughout her illness, or my pain after her death. My family's pattern was to attempt to mask suffering through activity. Of course this never works. Mom's illness shattered our family. We all were suffering but no one acknowledged it. If we had faced our fear and pain more openly we could have comforted each other. Our denial isolated us, and in some ways my family was never the same again.

Another level of this wound was my mother's broken heart. It was quite literally damaged. Yet I feel it was also troubled spiritually. At a certain point in her life my mother betrayed herself. She stopped using her creative gifts and tried to fit into the stuffy, high society of our hometown. I believe this betrayal of her true self contributed to her final illness.

The broken hearts in my story are powerful artifacts. As long as I denied the pain of my brokenness I couldn't receive the teaching it offered. It took me a long time to face how much my mother's death had affected me. It also took a long time to acknowledge my mom's betrayal of her gifts and how much that affected her. Yet the pain of these realizations is fertile ground for my healing.

My mother's broken heart taught me to cherish my authentic self and aspire to make all my choices from that place. I was given a chance to redeem what she denied for herself. Perhaps this is the beauty of brokenness— that we can take the pieces and create something new and meaningful.

My own broken heart taught me to embrace suffering. Thomas Merton once wrote in *New Seeds of Contemplation*, "The truth that many people never understand until it's too late, is that the more you avoid suffering the more you suffer." There is so much suffering in our world. Yet, I cannot open my heart to all that pain to the exclusion of my own brokenness. My spiritual challenge has been to gently balance the needs of my own heart with my yearning to engage the heart of all living things.

How do we find our way to that place where our brokenness turns to wholeness? What determines whether our heart will awaken or shut down? Mili's story is deeply instructive here. After constant heartbreak Mili reached out and asked for help. She realized that she needed others to help her heal her brokenness. Then she reached out even further to embrace God and her spirituality. Finally, she extended herself as a healer to help others in trouble. Each time she reached out she joined with the one big heart of creation, and drew strength from it. Her journey covers diverse terrain— hope and despair, progress and setbacks, and hard work and grace. Yet, here in the complexity of that terrain her story comes alive, she lives fully, and discovers that her brokenness is her connection to the unbroken whole

Each of us is broken in some way. Whether we find meaning in our suffering or give in to despair is crucial not only to our personal healing but also to the healing of our world. As we make sense of our own brokenness, then we can bring this wisdom to others. When we choose to pick up our broken pieces and make something new and authentic we all become stronger and more whole.

Exercise: Unearthing Your Broken Heart

Close your eyes, quiet your mind, and gently follow your breath until you begin to relax.

Now you are digging for the broken heart in your story: the experience that shattered you to the core.

A few thoughts before you begin this exercise. First you might want to review the work you did on your central image, as sometimes there is a relationship between your image and your broken heart. Secondly, if you are just starting to uncover the broken heart in your story it can be very scary and very painful. If this is a part of your story you have never thought much about before, you would be wise to do this exercise with a trusted friend, therapist, or family member. With their help you can move in gentle, gradual steps, uncovering just the amount of pain that you can bear. Remember the process of healing a broken heart takes time, loving support, and abundant courage. For those who have already done work to heal your broken heart you will find this exercise can move you to the next level of your healing.

The way you relate to your brokenness determines whether your heart awakens or closes, whether you find meaning in your suffering, or are lost in futility and despair. As painful as it is, your very brokenness is your connection to the unbroken whole. Place your hands on your heart and focus on the qualities of courage, openness, and a desire to awaken.

Now visualize your heart as broken and simply allow a free flow of images and words to come to you. What life experience, or experiences, broke your heart? How did you respond to your brokenness? With denial, despair, cynicism, cold detachment, collapsing into overwhelm, closing your heart to life, or using activity to cover feeling? Try to keep your heart open and feel the real pain of your brokenness. In feeling your pain you are preparing fertile ground for your healing. Take time to reflect, draw, and journal.

To find your way to that place where your brokenness turns to wholeness takes courage and a fierce desire to awaken. Working with these questions as honestly as possible will help. Do you passionately desire to awaken, to keep your heart open even though it has been shattered? Are you willing to get help, if you need to, in order to transform your brokenness? Can you turn to your spirituality to help you? What is the teaching in your broken heart? Are you willing to go beyond your own suffering and offer your learning to others? As you make sense of your own brokenness, offering it to something larger, you join the ever unfolding eternal story of what it means to be human. Remember, as you answer these questions be loving with yourself, take all the time you need, and get both human and spiritual support when you need it.

RADICAL SURPRISES THAT
WAKE US UP

The soul should always stand ajar.
—*Emily Dickinson*

It is astonishing how many of us have a vivid wake-up call in our story, a radical surprise that sets us spinning and profoundly affects how we understand ourselves and our role in life. Sometimes the surprise that awakens us comes in the form of an illness, divorce, or a long hidden secret. Though frequently painful, the surprises and wake-up calls in our stories are like hidden treasures, once uncovered they are full of healing power.

One night at the dinner table when I was about thirteen years old my parents were having a terrible fight. I can't remember what it was about, but at a certain moment my mother began to cry. So did my brother and sister and so did I. Then my father wept. He told us his own father had shot himself as he stood there watching. He had experienced this terrible abandonment when he was only twelve years old. My father said, in anguish, "All I ever wanted was for us to be happy." Then he left the dinner table. He never mentioned this loss to us again.

Many years later, as my father grew ill and frail, I visited him in the nursing home he hated. I wanted more than anything to talk about the mystery of my grandfather's suicide. I was desperate to know this part of my father's story. I planned what I would say over and over during the frequent four-hour drive. Yet, when I was finally there words wouldn't come. I was lost in the denial that had been with us for so long. In some ways I never really knew my father because he never revealed the nature of his suffering.

The radical surprise—that I would never know the significance of my grandfather's suicide, and its impact on my father and on our family—took no more than a few minutes at our dinner table. Yet my dreams, ever since, have been filled with a longing to understand my grandfather's decision to end his life. This surprise shocked me and woke up my lifelong search to understand suffering. My father's buried grief has inspired me to confront the suffering around me. It has taught me not to be afraid of the lacrimae rerum, the tears that are in all living things.

The mystery of my grandfather's suicide has been a catalyst in my life's work. Something I couldn't understand within my own story pushed me out to face the suffering of the world. We don't need to have every piece of an artifact to know whether it's a bowl or a spoon. I may never know the details of my father's anguish, yet I have come to understand how it affects my life. As you dig to reveal the hidden surprises in your story do so with mindfulness, gentleness, and the awareness that you need not find every part to understand the whole.

Fire and Water: Sonya's Story

After graduating from Vassar College, Sonya Shoptaugh moved to Washington, D.C., where she directed The Model Early Learning Center (MELC). MELC was a school that worked with low-income children and families, and it has been cited as a new vision of preschool education.

"People often ask me where do I get all my fire, all my passion? My father is an extremely passionate, creative person. He's a professional trumpet player and an inventor. I have so many wonderful memories of going to the symphony with him, and of discussing Emerson's essays on self-reliance. My dad pushes me and mentors me. My brain is working the hardest when I'm creating with my father.

"When my grandfather died, some years ago, my father and I sat together on the terrace of his home in the Oakland Hills. We had spectacular views of the mountains and we each had a glass of wine. My father looked at me and said, 'Whatever you love to do, do it now. Life is so precious, and so short. Don't hesitate.' I smiled and said, 'Dad, you've always told me that and I'm doing it right now.' The mandate from my father is so clear and passionate.

"My mom is the glue, the one who kept us all together. My father is very strong and creative, and he can be quite challenging. My mother did everything she could to make sure that we were a family. She established a sense of community for us. Holidays and birthdays were great ritual celebrations. Aunts, uncles, cousins, and grandparents were all there. Music was at the heart of our family celebrations, my dad at the trumpet, and my mom at the piano. My mom is sensitive to people's needs and she taught me that life is sustained in and through community. Her mandate came through in my life's work as an educator.

"With my dad I feel like I need to be on my toes. With mom I am totally relaxed, and I can let it all hang out. Tea times with my mom are so precious. I can talk about the silliest details of my life, that mean nothing in one sense, but still say everything. My mom brings me into the flow of things. She brings out the water, the sea of feeling and emotions.

"Fire and water. Sometimes I tease my parents because they offered me such different examples of how to live. Yet the tension of the opposites is what makes up the creative process. I have both sides. Sometimes they are in conflict. My spiritual challenge is to keep them in balance.

"I had a wake-up call in 1991 that literally compelled me to bring more water into my life. A California wildfire totally destroyed my childhood home of twenty-one years. Everything was gone, all the family photographs, the records of my dad's company, the house. It was devastating for our family. My rational mind couldn't understand something so big, and I began to ask deep spiritual questions about life.

"Shortly after the wildfire I almost burned down my house in Washington, D.C., and a few months later I caught on fire myself. This series of fires coming closer and closer woke me up spiritually. I started to see another dimension that I had ignored. I needed to take some time out, to pause, and look inward. I went to a friend's houseboat and surrounded myself with water. I'd had enough fire.

"Floating on the houseboat I had a series of dreams. I realized that the passion and fire I had for my work as an activist needed to be balanced with a passion for my spiritual evolution. The fire literally had come to tell me this was time for me to start looking inward. The spiritual journey I have taken since, allows me to relate in a much deeper and more balanced way to my social contributions.

"The fires also gave me an important lesson about wake-up calls. The wildfire that obliterated my childhood home created space for a whole new life. Another way of believing, another way of looking, another way of being. This terrible tragedy cleared the way and gave me the space to become something else. My whole family has changed because of the fire. The fire destroyed our home, and rebuilt our lives."

The movement of Sonya's life takes her from activism in the inner city of Washington, D.C., to the interior of her soul. Her wake-up call compelled her to care for her spiritual needs as well as her passion to contribute to a better society. She realized we need the in-breath as well the out-breath to live in balance with the natural rhythm of life.

Sonya's story is instructive in another way. On one level, a wake-up call often destroys something, on another level it offers the opportunity for something new to be born. I have seen this over and over again as my students face illness, death, divorce, or loss of a job. Though all these events are painful, they are also transformers. Wake-up calls can hit us hard. If we don't pay attention the fire comes closer and closer as Sonya found out. We can resist the wake-up call and suffer more, or we can use it to shake us out of our trance. Waking up we begin to live more authentically, we set new priorities so we can spend more time with our family, take care of our health, do nothing for awhile, or explore a new way to give back to society.

On a spiritual level a wake-up call is simply a reminder of the ephemeral nature of all life. In *When Things Fall Apart*, the Buddhist teacher, Pema Chodron, describes the opportunity inherent in these situations: "Life is a good teacher and a good friend. Things are always in transition, if we could only realize it. Nothing ever sums itself up in the way that we like to dream about. The off-center, in-between state is an ideal situation, a situation in which we don't get caught, and in which we can open our hearts and minds beyond limit." Most of us resist those moments when we feel off-balance. Yet only by entering them can we listen closely to our rhythm and once again find our equilibrium.

I invite you to pay attention when you feel off-balance— in your work, family, relationships, inner life, emotional or physical health. Maybe it's time for a change. Maybe a wake-up call is at your door—a reminder that life is always surprising us, teaching us, and preparing us for the final change at the end of life when we die.

Exercise: Uncovering the Radical Surprise

Close your eyes, quiet your mind, and gently follow your breath until you begin to relax.

As you continue your soul dig, you are searching for the wake-up call, the radical surprise that set you spinning and profoundly changed the way you see your life.

Review your life for the times you felt startled awake, shaken out of your trance, somehow changed. The most obvious wake-up calls are when you face illness, death, divorce, loss of a job, or a long hidden secret. As you dig to reveal the hidden surprises in your story do so with mindfulness, gentleness, and the awareness that you need not find every part to understand the whole. Simply allow a free flow of images and words to come to you. What is the radical surprise, or surprises, in your story? Take time to reflect, draw, and journal.

Now reflect on your life at this moment—your work, family, relationships, inner life, and emotional or physical health. Listen carefully to your rhythm. Are you seriously out of balance in any areas of your life? Is a wake-up call at your door asking you to pay attention, to make a change? What do you need to do to bring more balance into your life on a daily and weekly basis? Make an agreement with yourself to take the first steps.

Five

GATHERING THE PIECES INTO A WHOLE: OFFERING THE LESSONS IN YOUR STORY

Fate is encountered only by him that actualizes freedom. . . .
[H]e that puts aside possessions and cloak and steps bare
before the countenance—this free human being encounters
fate. It is not his limit but his completion; freedom and fate
embrace each other to form meaning; and given meaning,
fate—with its eyes, hitherto severe, suddenly full of light—
looks like grace itself.

—Martin Buber, from I and Thou

How do we allow freedom and fate to embrace each other so that we form meaning from our life stories? How do we gather the separate artifacts together and make a meaningful whole? We have learned that telling the truth about our stories is what allows freedom and fate to merge into meaning. When we stand naked with the pain of our core wound, the shadow of our mask, and fragility of our broken heart— indeed our fate can look like grace itself.

To transform the suffering in our stories into a meaningful experience requires a courageous heart and a keen spiritual alertness. This alertness steers us away from an endless addiction to our suffering. An alert spirit and a courageous heart help us avoid creating our entire identity from our wounds. These highly seductive forces can rob us of meaning and trap us in the dead end of narcissism. To stay clear of these pitfalls we need to respect our pain while avoiding self-indulgence.

Ultimately, for the fullest meaning to emerge from our story we need to offer our learning—both joy and sorrow—to a story larger than our own. By connecting the suffering in our story with the larger story of the human family and the earth, we achieve a sense of proportion and find our place in the vast scheme of life and find the grace inherent in our fate. At this intersection we find healing and spiritual wholeness, and we learn to offer the lessons of our story in service to others.

My spiritual wholeness has come as I learn to embrace my needs and imperfections, and to balance my passion for action with time for simply being with the beauty of the world. My mask of overachievement linked me to the collective overdrive of society: overconsumption, overpopulation, and overwhelming the earth. The broken heart and radical surprise in my story taught me that suffering would not go away by ignoring it. With my willingness to face suffering I learn how to hold the pain of others and respond creatively to the call of the world.

I began this work because I could no longer be effective in my efforts to contribute to the world until I confronted my own suffering. Sonya's story is similar to mine as she moves from her fiery passion to heal society into the deep waters of her own inner healing. Gary and Mili's stories take us from rich inner experiences out into the world. Gary's memory of stardust is his doorway to healing both people and the earth. The triumph of Mili's inner healing leads her to give back to society. Thus we feel the rhythm of compassion moving in and out, connecting us to the eternal rhythm of life.

Maud's Story: Trusting That the Pieces Will Fall into Place

Arrange whatever pieces come your way.
—*Virginia Woolf*

Mystics tell us that the truest joy is the fully lived life. The more richly we live, the more we come into rhythm with the eternal story. I saw this richness always in my eighteen-year friendship with Maud Morgan. As a young artist, living abroad, she formed friendships with James Joyce and Ernest Hemingway. When she was seventy-seven, she took a six-month trip through Africa—by herself. At ninety-two she wrote her memoirs, *Maud's Journey: A Life from Art*. She kept on growing right up to her death at ninety-six in 1999. Like all of our stories, Maud's was full of broken hearts, false masks, radical surprises, and spiritual challenges.

Maud's core challenge was to follow her calling as an artist. To stay true to her calling she had to live through a myriad of difficult experiences. For years she felt ill at ease with her family and battled feelings of inadequacy. For a while she even stopped painting and only after a painful divorce was she able to start a new life and return to her life's purpose. The lessons from her suffering and her joys infuse her art.

Like so many of us Maud strove to balance her inner life as an artist with her outer engagement in the world. In the 1980s during the height of the Cold War she chose to close her painting studio for some time and became a passionate antinuclear activist. For the last decade of her life she mentored young women painters and set up a fund in her name to support the work of aspiring artists. Maud told me that she went through with the challenging task of writing her memoirs because she hoped that others could learn from her life. Over the course of our friendship she was an outstanding role model of someone living fully, and offering the lessons of her story to serve others.

Maud lived on a quiet street in Cambridge, near Harvard Square. Whenever my work brought me to Boston, I would pay her a visit. It was a pilgrimage, really. I would always arrive with a huge bouquet of flowers. After Maud arranged them, we would sit together and have tea. Each time, I would lose myself in her extraordinary face. Nine decades of joys and sorrows wound their way through a vast array of wrinkles and lines, telling so many stories I could get dizzy looking at her. Her head was surrounded by a great shock of white hair. "I want to look like Albert Einstein," she once said.

On what would be my final visit, Maud's strength was declining, though her mind was as sharp as ever and her humor in rare form. "I am not dead yet so I thought I would have another show," she said to me. She was working on a new series of collages. She could cut out the pieces of the collage but her hands trembled too much to glue them in place. She'd recently hired a woman to serve as her apprentice. Maud lived in an A-frame structure with abundant light pouring in from windows in the ceiling. She set up her "studio" beside her bed. Maud said, "I've learned to be very careful with my precious energy, using it only for what I really love. Sometimes I sleep twelve hours at a stretch, then go right to my worktable. There is less difference," she explained, "between my dream and waking life. These two worlds are becoming seamless."

I watched Maud move her brightly colored shapes into a design. She said, "I don't know exactly what will emerge, I just trust that the pieces will fall into place." As she worked, I saw the fragments of her life and of my own and of all the stories I had heard begin to fall into a great, majestic order. Maud was right: The central images, the artifacts from our parents, the false masks, broken hearts, and radical surprises all come together in a unique design, a living whole. If only we can trust.

Maud's capacity to trust came from decades of mastering her art form, as well as decades of confronting the demons in her own life story. Towards the end of her memoir she says, "Now I end this story of a life like any other, both fragile and tough, the fragility evident from the start, the toughness formed en route. I'm kinder to myself now, less critical of the good and bad things that occur in the present or past. Maybe later I will start to worry about death and dying, but I haven't quite finished living enough yet to forfeit my spare time to apprehension."

Perhaps it is only with time that we cultivate the capacity to trust that our lives are unfolding just the way they need to. Maud taught me that this trust is nurtured by an unabashed desire to live fully, facing our fears and challenges and then getting on with it, finding what we love and doing it, and sharing what we've learned with the world.

As we conclude this section with the in-breath of self-understanding we ready ourselves to move to the out-breath of service. Moving out into the world our stories mature in vital new ways and our self-understanding deepens as we reach out to others.

PART II

The Out-Breath
Caring for the World

The best way to become a better "helper" is to become a better person. But one necessary aspect of becoming a better person is via helping other people. So one must and can do both simultaneously.

—Abraham Maslow, from Religions, Values,
and Peak Experiences

INTRODUCTION

We began our quest for self-understanding by realizing that we had to tell the truth about our personal story so that real healing could take place. It is the same with the world's story—we need to acknowledge certain truths as we start out.

In America today, some thirty-eight million people live in poverty, and many are single mothers and children. Ten percent of America's citizens control the vast majority of wealth, and the United States now has the greatest gap between the rich and poor of any industrialized country. Unless we change our consumption patterns we will be responsible for the extinction of 25 percent of all species by 2025. As a small 5 percent of the world's population, Americans consume one-third of the planet's resources. While we use up to three times more than our fair share, at least a billion people in our world aren't getting enough food to survive.

If we allow these statistics to register deep in our hearts, we cannot ignore them—not if we wish to consider ourselves people with moral integrity. When this inequity hits home emotionally and spiritually, something inside us shifts.

We aspire to become our brother and sister's and earth's keeper.

All spiritual traditions emphasize the mutually beneficial interchange between self-fulfillment and service to others— the in-breath and the out-breath. At the heart of this wisdom is the simple and profound understanding that we cannot ignore others' suffering, because they are part of us. If we isolate ourselves and disconnect from the suffering in the world, we are actually disconnecting from ourselves. This fragmentation is at the core of our spiritual emptiness in America today.

Visionaries like Martin Luther King, Dorothy Day, Thomas Merton, Aldo Leopold, Henry David Thoreau, Simone Weil, and Mahatma Gandhi have guided us toward a socially engaged spirituality. All made radical commitments to changing both the psyche and the world. The Dalai Lama is one of the most eloquent advocates for this integration. He says our vast global challenges can only be resolved by balancing our inner development with compassionate action.

In his Nobel Peace Prize acceptance speech, "A Call for Universal Responsibility," the Dalai Lama says "Because we all share this small planet earth, we have to learn to live in harmony and peace with each other and with nature. That is not just a dream, but a necessity. We are dependent upon each other in so many ways that we can no longer live in isolated communities and ignore what is happening outside."

At this critical time in history, we face unprecedented challenges including overpopulation, poverty, violence, and ecological destruction. Ten days before the visionary inventor Buckminster Fuller died, he asked this question, "Whether humanity is to continue and prosper on spaceship Earth depends entirely on the integrity of the human individuals and not on the political and economic systems. The cosmic question has been asked, are humans a worthwhile invention?" My deepest conviction is that we can prosper, by joining the exploration of consciousness with a passion to contribute to the world.

The spirit of service has always been a rich part of the American character. Whether responding to the many recent natural disasters, the terrible bombing in Oklahoma City, or the tragic murders in Littleton, Colorado, Americans take pride in caring for one another. Some of us are motivated by spiritual or religious aspirations, others by political beliefs, and many by the personal fulfillment that comes from caring for others. In this section of the book, we chart the aspects of service that nourish our souls and profoundly connect us to the human family and this precious planet of ours. We experience the truth of Dr. Martin Luther King's words, "Everyone can be great because everyone can serve."

In the chapters ahead we'll engage with the suffering in the world as spiritual inquiry—wrestling with it, being humbled by it, and most of all allowing it to deepen our compassion. As we enter the story of society and the earth we continue with our archaeological metaphor, this time digging for the awakened heart. We are searching to uncover the tools of compassion that open our hearts, helping us to see the true nature of suffering. This awakened heart allows us to respond skillfully to our planetary challenges.

In digging for the awakened heart there will again be four phases of excavation:

1. *preparing the ground for conscious service*—you learn to follow your rhythm of compassion choosing when to serve and the kind of service that's right for you

2. *uncovering your social shadow*—you learn to expose the burden of moral prescription that destroys authentic caring—shame, guilt, shoulds, and spiritual arrogance
3. *unearthing the four qualities of mature compassion: a quiet mind, an open heart, presence, and radical simplicity*—you move through your shadow to a place of effortless generosity where serving flows naturally and freely
4. *discovering service and stewardship as an extension of spiritual practice*—you learn to open so fully to suffering that your heart breaks in a way that liberates you and illuminates the invisible pain of the world.

In each of these four phases you will use the insights from your personal story to help you connect with the world's story. You will see how your story comes into full bloom as you encounter the world.

Six

PREPARING THE GROUND FOR CONSCIOUS SERVICE

Compassion in action is paradoxical and mysterious. It is
absolute yet continually changing. It accepts that everything
is happening exactly as it should, and it works with a full-
hearted commitment to change. It is joyful in the midst of
suffering, and hopeful in the face of overwhelming odds. It is
simple in a world of complexity and confusion. It is done for
others, but it nurtures the self. It intends to eliminate suffering, knowing that suffering is limitless.

—*Ram Dass, from* Compassion in Action

Over the years, hundreds of students have come to my
classes searching for ways to balance self-fulfillment with service to others. These seekers have come to understand that
with spiritual maturity comes the capacity to go beyond one-
self and to embrace another's suffering. Yet our encounters
have also made it clear to me how complex social contribution can be.

Along with their eagerness to serve, my students are asking important questions. How do I balance the urgent needs
of our times with my own need to care for myself? If I choose

not to serve, am I taking care of myself or has my personal drama or spiritual laziness seduced me? How do I find time to serve? How do I open to my generosity, to my natural desire to give without shame, should, or guilt?

I designed a major component of my "Grace Spiritual Growth Training Program" to address these inquiries and explore the nature of conscious service. I called this part of the training "A Compassionate Encounter with Suffering." To begin, I asked the students to choose an area of service that would help them deepen their compassion. The idea was to move into a situation where their heart breaks, using the mantra "my heart is breaking, my heart is awakening." In leaving our comfort zones we would find a fuller connection to the human family and the natural world. I was asking a lot. The response and the learning were remarkable. Over a period of six years, my students documented their work with battered women, homeless people, holocaust survivors, prisoners, racial healing, abused animals, endangered forests, toxic waste dumps, the elderly, the handicapped, hospices, people with AIDS, and much more.

For the most part we exchanged our experience by reading excerpts from our service journals, which will form much of the content for the following chapters. Sometimes we illuminated the insights from our service through painting, sculpture, photography, poetry, dance, or drama presentations. At times there was such unbearable pain and heartbreak in our sharing that I wondered if I'd gone too far. But I hadn't. We grew strong together.

We taught one another that our hearts were capable of far more compassion than we had ever imagined. Sometimes we had to go through fear, confusion, and resistance to arrive at that place. Often our caring was messy, complex, and full of shadow. We found that moral prescription—feeling burdened by shame, guilt, or shoulds—destroys the true joy of giving, and that more and more our service arose from effortless generosity. We learned that we were personally healed in profound and inexplicable ways through serving others. It is my hope that our stories will offer you some of this learning.

The first phase of excavation in digging for the awakened heart is to prepare the ground for conscious service. This is much like the commitment to tell the truth as a precondition for the healing that comes from our personal stories. Here too there are several preconditions that prepare the way for the awakened heart: defining what service is; learning to follow our rhythm of compassion so that we balance self-care while we engage in service; and choosing the area of service that's appropriate for us.

DEFINING SERVICE

I had begun to see how complicated this notion of service is, how it is a function not only of what we do but who we are (which of course, gives shape to what we do).
—*Robert Coles, from* The Call of Service

Service can manifest both in formal volunteering such as serving in soup kitchens or prisons, replanting forests, or helping in a shelter for battered women, and through informal channels: the office worker who goes out of her way to listen to a colleague in crisis; the father who coaches his son's basketball team as a form of mentoring; the restaurant owner who sends her compost to an organic farm or makes sure all of her leftover food goes to homeless shelters; the couple who takes in an aging parent rather than send them to a nursing home. We need all these acts of loving kindness to build the kind of communities that we hope for.

Sometimes we manifest our service within our vocation: the teacher who makes sure he builds the self-esteem of all his students; the business owner who treats each of her employees and customers with respect and kindness; the publisher who makes a commitment to using renewable resources (soy inks, paper from companies with sustainable timber practices) or aspires to bring books into the world that add inspiration and value to people's lives. The issues discussed in this section are intended for anyone—parent, social worker, businessperson, or concerned citizen—who desires to care in a more conscious and loving way.

We also need to remember that our capacity to serve changes with the different cycles of our life. The generation in their twenties is brimming with idealism and longs to channel their moral passion out in the world; they may join the Peace Corps or Teach for America, or Greenpeace. Later, our caring may take the form of conscious parenting, serving on school committees, and coaching Little League. As the children grow older, serving as a family—in a nursing home, a soup kitchen, or planting trees in the community—offers the children important values and teaches them that giving is a form of self-fulfillment. When the kids leave home, middle-aged couples often discover a deep yearning to give back to society. They may use their vacation to work for Habitat for Humanity or to start a mentoring program for inner-city teens or to travel as eco-tourists.

In addition to these broad cycles, we need to continue the ongoing practice of balancing our own self-care with the care of the world. My students range in age from their late twenties to their midseventies. No matter what phase of life they are in, they are all looking to balance their own needs with the needs of those they serve. As we saw in Part One, without the in-breath of self-reflection we can't sustain our involvement with the suffering of the world. Now we continue our exploration into the necessity of balance to insure the clarity of heart and mind required for the complex challenges of service.

LISTENING TO YOUR RHYTHM OF COMPASSION

The time for contemplation is the spring that feeds our action, and our action will be as deep as the spring. We need time to allow the spirit to clear the obstacles—the clinging debris and mud—that keeps the spring from flowing freely from its clear, deep source. And we need time for the spring to overflow into insightful and compassionate action.

—Thomas Merton

The second part of preparing the ground for conscious service is learning to follow your rhythm of compassion: Knowing when it's time to be on the in-breath, caring for self, or on the out-breath, caring for the needs of the world. Being in rhythm, capable of balancing your inner and outer impulses, is a precondition of mature compassion for society and the earth. An ongoing practice I use with my students is to ask them to really listen to their rhythm. Where is compassion leading me at this time in my life—inward towards personal needs, or outward paying more attention to my role in the world?

A talented social worker specializing in drug and alcohol abuse counseling discovers he's burned out and needs to take time off for renewal. A mother who's active with a multitude of volunteer activities in her community worries that her teenage daughter is increasingly depressed and alienated. She drops some of her community activities to spend more time with her daughter. A dedicated wetlands ecologist takes time off for the first time in many years to be rejuvenated by the natural world she's working so hard to protect. These people find their rhythm of compassion by focusing on the in-breath.

A busy lawyer spends one less late evening at the office and instead volunteers at an AIDS hospice. Later he asks his teenage son to join him, and their relationship deepens to new levels. A therapist feels empty and disconnected from the world. Rather than leading another group for her clients, she volunteers her skills at the local shelter for battered women. A college professor takes one less afternoon in the research library and finds fulfillment working outdoors cleaning up a local river. To balance their lives these people needed to focus on the out-breath.

Let's explore how to follow our rhythm of compassion from several perspectives. First, we'll examine busyness as the great trickster of balance—stealing from the person who never has time to contribute to society, or seducing the activist into never having time to care for herself. Then we'll discuss belonging to our place, putting down deep roots where we live as the sturdy anchor of balance, giving us the grounding to listen to our rhythm. Finally we'll look at the friends of balance—imagination, discipline, and support—the qualities that help us skillfully follow our rhythm of compassion.

Busyness: The Trickster of Balance

A major block to finding our rhythm is that we're often too busy to listen to where compassion is guiding us. So many of my students longed to make a more meaningful contribution to the world, but many found they had no time. Others were dedicated activists and found no time for their own lives. In classes and workshops, we study the following passage from Thomas Merton as a way to be sensitive to our rhythm of compassion. It is a reminder to those of us who are overextended activists addicted to service, and to those who are addicted to busyness and never have time to serve.

> The rush and pressure of modern life are a form, perhaps the most common form, of innate violence. To allow oneself to be carried away by a multitude of conflicting concerns, to surrender to too many demands, to commit oneself to too many projects, to want to help everyone in everything is to succumb to violence. The frenzy of the activist neutralizes his work for peace. It destroys her own inner capacity for peace. It kills the root of inner wisdom that makes work fruitful.

These words point to the very heart of our spiritual bankruptcy. In his book, *Time and Soul,* Jacob Needleman says "The time famine of our lives and our culture is in fact a symptom of metaphysical starvation." Many of us in America live abundant lives. Yet we are like the knight Parsifal standing before the Grail Castle, seeing the most beautiful court in the world, and forgetting to ask the most important question: Whom does the Grail serve? In modern terms we have to ask: In all this abundance, what matters most? How am I spending my time? Am I using it compassionately and creatively? What goals does my spirit serve?

So often we're on automatic pilot, going to the office each day, earning a living, car-pooling the kids, trying to keep up with the demands of ordinary life. But when do we step back and recognize the harm we do to ourselves and others by living such frenetic lives? My students all longed to make a more meaningful contribution to society, but many found they had no time. They too began to realize the violence of their busy lives. Dwight is a Harvard graduate and a gifted management consultant. This excerpt from his service journal describes the dilemma many of us face.

How inadequate I feel! I am so afraid of suffering that I cannot even begin to choose an area of service. I don't want to be melodramatic but part of my problem has been my unwillingness to even approach the subject. Said another way, "How I have suffered over suffering!" My agony is a mixture of impotence and fear.

Now I'm ready to face the fear, yet there is no time. Time, and how I use it, is at the heart of my spiritual exploration. As I examine my use of time it leads me to many dark places. I am seeing that I keep myself incessantly busy so I can avoid the hard areas in my life. How well-defended I am. Is it even worth trying?

To approach the issue of society's suffering I first have to deal with why I've chosen to stay so busy. I need to find out why I have no time for something so important to me.

Dwight's story is a stirring example of the destructiveness of a busy life. He had no time for many of the things that really mattered to him, and further he had no time to feel. He used his particular false mask—the in-demand consultant, the workaholic—to avoid his own suffering. Before Dwight could reach out to society he needed to take the in-breath and face his own demons.

The death of Dwight's mother offered him a potent wake-up call. Through her death he faced his fears about suffering and reevaluated his life priorities. His mother died at home and Dwight was her loving caretaker during her final days. The quiet dignity of her death, infused with poignant memories of her full and meaningful life, provided a mirror for Dwight to see his current life choices with stark reality.

Dwight was wise enough to heed his wake-up call and he began to make some changes. Shortly after his mother's death he went into counseling and strengthened his spiritual practice. He joined a support group that helped him make the lifestyle changes he desired. His healing process was neither quick nor easy. He once told me that changing his life to make room for what really mattered was like turning an oil tanker. Yet after several years his inner work is taking firm hold; he's working less and spending more time with his family, and he's found ways to reach out by mentoring others.

Many of my students found that busyness, at work and at home, was often a defense against deeply buried wounds. It kept them from what really mattered and the longing to contribute something back to the world. In slowing down they could address and heal these painful places. As they cleared the decks, to make time for either service or their own self-nourishment, many found they could do with a lot less. Less work, less television and e-mail, less talking and overanalysis, less stimulation, and less noise. They also made fewer dates and phone calls, and decided to forego social situations that left them feeling empty or indifferent. What a relief it is to clear away the things that drain our energy and make room for what nourishes us. Now we have the space to really hear our rhythm of compassion.

Exercise: Clearing the Decks

In your journal do a written review of the way you spend a typical week. Include both your outer contributions as well as your inner self-care. Write down everything as it actually is, try not to censor yourself. Then ask yourself which inner and outer activities are necessary and life giving? Which ones nourish and renew me? Take time to reflect, draw, and journal.

Now ask which activities—inner and outer—can I eliminate or reduce? Which ones drain my energy and leave me feeling empty or indifferent? The trickster busyness is very sly here and will try to convince you that everything is necessary. Here are some hints about what you can eliminate or reduce: work, food, television, e-mail, phone calls, talking and overanalysis, complaining, self-absorption, stimulation, noise, unnecessary dates, and constantly doing for others. Make a commitment to start eliminating at least one unnecessary activity this week, and then commit to one more for the next four weeks.

Belonging to Place: The Roots of Balance

We have forgotten what we can count on. The natural world provides refuge. . . . Each of us harbors a homeland, a landscape we naturally comprehend. By understanding the dependability of place, we can anchor ourselves as trees.
      —*Terry Tempest Williams, from* An Unspoken Hunger

If busyness is the sly trickster trying to upset balance, then belonging to our place, putting down deep roots where we live, is the sturdy anchor of balance. Belonging to our place—be it urban or rural—provides the literal grounding for our rhythm of compassion. Our place is the presence that witnesses us and provides us refuge.

Belonging to a place is not only a primary aspect of caring for the earth, it's also a fundamental need for spiritual well-being. It's both personal and political. I often tell my students that knowing the details of their home landscape is as important as knowing the details of their life story. Without a sense of place we are rootless with no ground to grow in. And herein lies part of the loss of soul in modern life. When we lose our attachment to place we lose our grounding. Genuine belonging to place allows us to belong to ourselves, to be rooted in our rhythm, knowing when to pay attention to self and when to focus on the world.

Knowing the details of our place develops mindful intimacy, the opposite of disconnected busyness. We stop and notice the sight of the willow tree in our yard turning an incandescent autumn yellow, the dusk sounds of the birds in the park across from our apartment, the feel of the stone wall we have built along our driveway, the healing refuge of the small brook down the street, the smells of our beloved garden whether it be half an acre in the country or a tiny roof top plot in the city. As we come to know a place—the trees, plants, creatures, stones, water, and how they change with the light and shadow of the day and the cycles of the seasons—these elements combine into a strong network of attachment. Whether it is in the country, city, or suburbia this attachment is what makes a place a home and provides the foundation for a balanced rhythm.

Whether we live in the county or the city we can create a sense of place as we mindfully walk every inch of our surroundings, feed the birds, plant indigenous herb gardens, know the trees and creatures as we know our neighbors, study the maps and history of our region, or write love poems about our home landscape.

Until I left home for college I was blessed to live in one place where I formed a deep sense of attachment. College was followed by my gypsy years when I traveled the world and lived in many spots. When David and I got married we moved to the Hudson River Valley where we found a magical home nestled between the Southern Catskills and Shawangunk Mountains. After we'd lived in our home for about five years, a gifted palmreader told me that the lines in my hands reflected that I didn't really belong anywhere yet and that I needed to make a home for myself. He suggested that this was essential for my well-being. I immediately rejected his information as irrelevant, citing my beloved mountain home. Only years later did I understand what he had meant.

During the first five years in our home I was traveling internationally almost constantly. Working for world peace and involved with a myriad of citizen diplomacy projects, I lived in my house but I didn't belong to a home or a place. When I started my spiritual counseling right after my father's death part of my healing was to fall in love with the place where I lived. As I understood my overactivity as a distorted way to get love, I slowed down and traveled less. Staying home more, I became a passionate hiker in the mountains where I lived. I devoured the folklore and maps of my region. I learned that the Esophus Indians who lived along the Esophus Creek first inhabited these bluestone and shale mountains. They called the region *Ashokan*, or the place of many fishes.

Our mountain home has breathtaking views of the Ashokan Reservoir and the southern range of the Catskills. There they stand— Ashokan Highpoint, South, Table, Lone, Balsam Cap, Slide, the Wittenberg, Indian Head, and Overlook—venerable guardians watching over us. As I became more intimate with these mountains I began to call them the Grandmothers. At first I named them Grandmothers in honor of their ancient geological lineage with their shape like a primitive Goddess lying on her side—sensual, strong, and elegant. Later I realized these mountains had become my grand-mother. I lost all my physical grandparents before I was a teenager and over the years the presence of these mountains has offered me the wisdom and constancy of an elder.

I've come to know the Grandmothers in their many moods and seasons: hiking in the golden brilliance of autumn; snowshoeing in the silent white powder of winter; overjoyed by the unfolding chartreuse of spring; and remembering my childhood as I gather flowers and blueberries in the summer. In these mountains I know the presence of deer, rabbit, blue heron, and owl as I know my human neighbors. With time I've come to belong to the place where I live, it is a part of me and I am a part of it.

In recent years a recurring dream has visited me. I dream that I am an Esophus Indian woman asleep by the Kanape Brook on the Ashokan Highpoint trail. Then I awake as myself. The feeling in the dream is as if my own body emerges out of hers. The site of this dream is one of my favorite mountain trails where David and I hike several times a year as a small pilgrimage to the Grandmothers. I experience this dream as a gift of having finally come home to my true rhythm.

There are few things in life as steadfast as our place. It is our ground for meaning. As I learned to live in harmony with the seasons and cycles of my place, I began to live in harmony with my own rhythm. I could return to the refuge of my place to attune to my changing rhythms. I realized the roots of caring for place, self, and others are bound together as in a great tree.

Exercise: Rooting Yourself in Your Place

This exercise can be done anywhere in the place you live. If you live in a city it's helpful to do this exercise in the nearest park or natural environment. With journal and drawing materials go out your front door and walk around your neighborhood. Walking with a quiet mindful rhythm, be aware of as many details as possible: trees, creatures, birds, plants, stones, water, sky, people, and buildings. Pay attention with all your senses to the light, sounds, smells, shapes, colors, and textures. After walking for fifteen minutes pause to reflect, draw, and journal about the details that constitute your place.

Try mindfully walking around your neighborhood several times a week for the next few months. Be aware what happens when you walk in your place on a day when you are feeling sad or out of sorts, or a day when you feel great. Can you experience your place witnessing you, providing you refuge? Perhaps you'll want to plant an indigenous herb garden, or feed the birds, or write a love poem about your landscape. Notice that the more you practice mindfulness in your home landscape the more you belong to your place. And pay attention to your sense of belonging to yourself as you become more intimate with your place.

The Friends of Balance: Imagination, Discipline, and Support

The qualities of imagination, discipline, and support are the friends of balance, helping us find and sustain our rhythm.

In watching certain friends who seem to gracefully juggle family, self-care, work, and social and environmental causes, it's their ingenuity that strikes me. Getting their kids and spouses involved with their volunteer work at the local teen center combines caring for society with rich family time. Organizing everyone at the office to donate clothes, tools, furniture, and time to families who have been devastated by a fire boosts the morale at work and helps people in need. Setting up a recycling program at work makes environmental awareness a daily habit. For one of my students gardening is her deepest form of renewal. She and her daughter spend precious hours gardening together, and they give much of the fresh produce to the local soup kitchen. Imagination gets us out of the box, beyond the limitations of our ordinary routines.

For most of us—the busy doctor, harried executive, dedicated activist, or overextended parent—finding our rhythm is a creative juggling act where we gradually find the particular ingredients for balancing inner and outer. Carol Elizabeth learned to be an imaginative juggler when she became a city councilor. This entry from her service journal describes the qualities that help her weave together her need for spiritual nourishment with her many social concerns.

I am aspiring to be a city councilor from a place of compassion. I am also aspiring to be compassionate to myself. This arena of public service is complex, with so many dramas, wars, and witless whines. Far too much to do for too few councilors. Each day we face something crucial: capital budgets, arts and culture, greenspace, garbage, fire stations, safety and security—deciding the fortunes of workers at City Hall, which guns the police are to have, the future of parklands, the repair and maintenance of streets and sewers.

As I serve at City Hall I try to find the truth. Where the hell is it? I find distortions, deceptions, and manipulations. I find new rules and new games. It's hard to play along, but it's also hard not to. Can I encounter these paradoxes and games with compassion? I pray, I do battle, I withdraw, and I gently advocate. There are moments I am exactly where I need to be: writing the mission statement for the city; advocating for Council to meet privately without press or staff so we can speak our truth; educating people to reduce, recycle, and reuse not out of guilt but out of love for this small planet; presenting the Capital Budget as investment in our future and an antidote to cynicism.

All the while I am also learning to take care of myself. Certain things help a lot. Laughing at myself and drawing on a sense of humor. Praying before, during, and after council meetings. Asking my friends and constituents for advice, input, and support. Within my close circle of friends I give myself permission to cry, rage, pout, and yell about the enormous pressures of this job. With these dear ones I allow myself to be loved, cherished, and nourished.

I need to be vigilant about giving myself days off, tending to my soul and taking family time—about finding my in-breath with regular massages, meditation, kayaking, by taking a Sabbath day and turning off the phones. At the Council, I am learning to lead and cooperate, to be strong and vulnerable. I am learning this requires wakefulness not exhaustion.

We see Carol Elizabeth's imagination as she juggles soul and society. Her creativity brings together the ingredients of her unique rhythm of compassion—City Hall, capital budgets and greenspace, humor, prayer, educating people about the environment, time for catharsis, caring for her body, kayaking, vision as an antidote to cynicism, and solitude. We notice the wisdom of her imagination has brought forward a natural integration of body, mind, spirit, and heart.

The ingredients of our rhythms of compassion are as varied as our chosen forms of self-renewal: poetry, dance, silent retreat, time in the mountains or by the sea, long distance running, reading, solitude, singing in a choir, or playing an instrument. They are as infinitely diverse as we are in our chosen areas of contribution—education, conservation, drug rehabilitation, child abuse, racism, hunger, overpopulation, human rights, or endangered species. In the next part of this chapter we'll further discuss how to choose the right path of service. The creative challenge is to call upon your imagination and let it guide you to the particular combination that integrates the inner and the outer for you.

Along with ingenuity Carol Elizabeth shows us the role of discipline in juggling self-care with dedicated action. Since discipline often conjures up negative associations, it's helpful to think of it as rhythm with a purpose, the structure that gives us freedom. Unless we're disciplined in setting our priorities we've seen that the trickster busyness will run away with what matters to us. Like most of us with busy lives, Carol Elizabeth had to carefully carve out time for massage, meditation, or family time. She made quality of life a priority and then she guarded it ferociously. This required vigilance, the "just do it" mantra.

Finally, this story demonstrates the essential need for support in balancing our lives. This sounds so simple, but so many of us are stuck in the superhuman syndrome trying to do everything, and doing it all alone. This is often caused by our mask of perfectionism that we know puts up the false facade of loneliness, perfection, and independence. Carol Elizabeth was wise enough to ask for help and input from friends and constituents both for her work at City Hall as well as her self-care. She also had a close community of friends who offered her spiritual and emotional nourishment. In Dwight's story we saw the crucial role of support as he found a counselor and a support group to help him make his lifestyle changes. Support can come in many forms: a therapist or spiritual director, a twelve-step program, a men's group, a mentor in your chosen field of service, a trusted family member, friend, or colleague.

Throughout the last twenty years I have been part of a women's support group that has given me unflinchingly honest feedback about when I am burnt out, stuck in perfectionism, or in need of self-renewal. With these cherished women I have also laughed so hard I thought I'd burst; enjoyed some of the most decadent, delicious times of my life; and experienced the rare, complex, and mysterious process of authentic friendship. I am also close to a beloved community of friends who come together for meditation, silence, support, and celebration. I consider these circles of support among the most precious blessings in my life. There is no doubt in my mind that without their support I would not find my rhythm of compassion.

Our rhythms are as varied as Bach and the Beatles. Some of us tend to serve too much and get burnt out. We need to pay attention to taking time for self-renewal. Some of us are addicted to busyness and we need to clear the decks and find out what really matters to us. Others have spent too much time focused on their own self-care and are looking to move out into the world.

There's no right or wrong here, rather an invitation to listen intently to your rhythm and find out which direction compassion is leading you. This requires imagination to guide you to the unique ingredients of your rhythm; discipline to help you carve out the space for quality of life and then take a stand for it; and support to guide, reflect, and nourish you. And we need to recognize that this balance of inner and outer is an ongoing practice—sometimes we're in rhythm, sometimes we're not.

As you continue your work as a spiritual archaeologist you are now digging for the tools of compassion that awaken the heart. The first phase of your excavation is to find your rhythm of compassion so that you know when it's time to be on the in-breath, caring for self; or on the out-breath, caring for the needs of the world. Learning to listen to your rhythm is much like the sacred agreement you made to tell the truth as a precondition to finding your personal story. Being in rhythm—capable of balancing your inner and outer impulses—is a precondition to the awakened heart.

The following exercise will help you explore your rhythm of compassion. At the conclusion of the book you'll be invited to look at your rhythm once again, using the additional insights from the chapters ahead.

Exercise: Finding Your Rhythm of Compassion

Note to the reader: As with the other exercises in this book, this one is intended as an ongoing practice. Finding your rhythm of compassion may take weeks, or even months. Don't expect instant results. Be gentle with yourself, and return to this and other exercises as often as you like. Your "answers" will undoubtedly grow and deepen over time.

Close your eyes, quiet your mind, and gently follow your breath until you begin to relax.

Take a deep breath. More than anything else, finding your rhythm is a creative process. First bring your imagination forward and let it lead you to your unique ingredients of balancing self-renewal with contribution. Look at the list you made, earlier in this chapter, of the inner and outer activities that nourish and renew you. Ask, How can I get out of the box of my ordinary routines and let my ingenuity combine some of these preferred activities? Social contribution and family time? Self-care with family time? Offering my special talents to someone in need? Organizing my colleagues at work to recycle and reuse or to help out society? Take time to reflect, draw, and journal.

Now using all your insights from this exercise call on your imagination and let it guide you to a vision where you balance self-care with service to the world. Pay attention to whether you need to focus more on the in-breath or more on the out-breath at this cycle in your life. Write down exactly what your vision would look like.

As you set the inner and outer priorities in your vision where do you need to be especially vigilant—making sure you carve out time for what matters most to you? Which of your priorities do you need to carefully protect? Write these down and reflect on them for a few moments.

Be aware that your mask of perfectionism may try to sabotage you into believing that you can do everything, all alone. Make a commitment to finding the support you need to help you balance your life.

When you have finished this exercise take some time to reflect and read it over. Give yourself time to digest all the information you've uncovered. And remember, finding your rhythm of compassion is an ongoing practice—sometimes we're in rhythm, sometimes we're not. Often we learn the most when we're not in rhythm; stuck in burnout or self-obsession we experience the healing of paying more attention to where we need to focus our energies. No matter where we are in finding our rhythm, being loving and non-judgmental toward ourselves is always the most helpful attitude.

CHOOSING THE PATH THAT'S RIGHT FOR YOU

Once we've learned to pay attention to our rhythm we're ready for the final aspect of preparing the ground for conscious service—choosing the appropriate path of contribution. Advises Mirabai Bush in *Compassion in Action: Setting Out*

On The Path of Service: "Be brave, start small, use what you've got, do something you enjoy, don't overcommit." This sentence says it all and speaks of Mirabai's years of devoted activism as well as her wisdom in assisting others to find their way.

I use Mirabai's advice as the guideline for helping my students choose their arena of service. First of all recognize that if you're just starting out it takes courage to face the challenges of the world. Begin with a level of commitment that's appropriate for your life cycle. Look for something that calls out to you. Go back to the place of belonging in your life story for clues as to where you might want to contribute. For instance both my citizen diplomacy work and my environmental activism grew out of my deep sense of belonging with the earth. Then begin slowly, working one day or even a few hours a month perhaps, and gradually adding more hours as you get into the flow of it. One of the biggest mistakes people make when they start out is to overcommit.

It also may take some time to find the right fit between your talents and interests and a particular arena of service. In this journal entry, George begins to explore the right avenue for his contribution. George is a high-level computer consultant whose children have grown, and he's entered the cycle of life where he wants to give back to his community.

I thought, I want to do good work. I want to give both time and money to help others, so I set out eagerly to research the possibilities: Big Brothers, prisons, mental hospitals, hospices, and soup kitchens.

I was surprised at how difficult it was to find my place to give. The mental hospital seemed a good place to start, but the difficulty of phone calls, meetings, application forms, and training programs convinced me otherwise. Then I found a soup kitchen. Meals for the poor and homeless. In the schoolyard, all kinds of people lined up to be served. A bag lady. Young toughs. A man in suit and tie. Former mental patients released to the streets by cutbacks. I saw families dressed in their Sunday best take their places at old cafeteria tables. We said, "No big helpings or seconds please, until everyone has been served." And they answered, "Thank you, God bless you." As orderly as a theater ticket line. But more polite.

A good thing by a lot of people I thought. Businesses gave food to a food bank. The food bank gave to the soup kitchen. The Church gave the meeting place. We helped with cooking, serving, table setup and takedown, dishwashing, and trash pickup.

But, for me, something was not right. I was trying to learn compassion but I was not relating to people, only to stereotypes. To a bag lady. To a young tough. To a man in a suit. I could not feel the people behind these images.

They liked me there because I did good work. But it was not done with compassion. I examined my motivation. I was brought up to believe, if I do good, I will be good. Being good, I will be accepted, recognized, and loved. And I will receive the Big Reward. Heaven and some kind of giant, unending spiritual orgasm.

George demonstrates that it's often a process of trial and error before we find our appropriate path of service. Sometimes the bureaucracy involved is too much to deal with, other times we realize it's just not where we want to be. For example, you may be interested in doing hospice work but find you're uncomfortable with illness. Instead, you help out at a center for troubled teens and find a real fit for your talents and love of this age group. After some more exploring George found his place as an Alternatives to Violence Trainer in the Colorado State Prison System.

Working in prison offered George both stimulating challenge and opportunity to deepen in compassion. He felt he could give his best in this setting and learn invaluable lessons about life not available in the business world. The following exercise is designed for those who are searching for an appropriate area of service.

Exercise: Uncovering the Path That's Right for You

Close your eyes, quiet your mind, and gently follow your breath until you begin to relax. Focus on Mirabai Bush's advice:

- be brave
- start small
- use what you've got
- do something you enjoy
- don't overcommit.

Take your time to concentrate on each phrase and how it relates to you.

Ask yourself, What talents do I have to offer others? What kinds of things do I most enjoy doing that can help others? What kind of things do I know I don't like to do? What do I want to get out of my service to others? Paying attention to my rhythm of compassion, how much time can I realistically commit to my service? Take time to reflect, draw, and journal.

Using your insights from these questions ask what area of society calls out to me to make a contribution? List several places you would like to start your research. Some possibilities to stimulate your thinking—education, conservation, drug rehabilitation, child abuse, hospice, prisons, racism, hunger, community gardens, domestic violence, human rights, sustainable living, or endangered species. Go back to the place of belonging in your life story for clues as to where you might like to contribute.

What are the first steps you need to take to research this area of service? Make a commitment to take the first steps in the next two weeks. Remember, it might take some time to find the right fit for your skills and interests.

Seven

UNCOVERING THE SHADOW
SIDE OF SERVICE

> If we were going to forbid hypocrites to work here with us,
> there'd be no one to do the work, and no one to do the for-
> bidding! Each day we try to do the best we can—for all our
> faults and imperfections.
>
> —*Dorothy Day, from* The Long Loneliness

As George was searching for his appropriate path of service
he also started to struggle with deeper issues. He questioned
how he was relating to the people in the soup kitchen. Then
he looked at his motivation and his lack of real compassion
or connection with the people he was meeting. He didn't like
what he found. George introduced us to the shadow side of
service, the next major area of excavation in digging for the
awakened heart. In telling our personal stories we saw that it
was essential to face the shadow of our central image and our
false mask in order to find true self-understanding. To contribute to society in a true and lasting way we also need to
uncover our social shadow, exposing the burden of moral prescription that destroys authentic caring: shame, guilt,
shoulds, and spiritual arrogance.

Often we think that making a social contribution is straightforward. We choose an area and then jump in. The honeymoon phase goes like this: "This is wonderful! I feel good about myself and I am making a difference in the world." But then like George you may soon find yourself confronting a maze of intense and conflicting impulses. You may be startled to discover your need for self-esteem, approval, status, and power, all mixed up with your genuine desire to help. Some of us are shocked at our feelings of fear, repulsion, boredom, or perfectionism as we set out to serve. As we look deeper we may uncover the guilt, shame, or shoulds that motivate our caring. Others discover a martyr complex that says, "I can never do enough; if I stop serving, the world will fall apart."

The shadow side of service often has to do with wanting to "fix" a person or an issue. We want to feel more powerful, in control, be the expert, or play God. Here we're walking the fine line between compassion and condescension. At the heart of this is the illusion that we are different or separate from those we serve. Whether we are activists, managers, therapists, or parents, if our contribution is fueled by this insidious illusion, little genuine caring will take place and we will fail to receive the joy and fulfillment of conscious service.

Other common shadows include becoming a service workaholic, using your addiction to service as an excuse not to examine your own feelings and your own need for balance. Or giving into cynicism and despair—belief that the world is going to the dogs and that nothing can be done about it. You go through the motions, all the while feeling nothing you do really makes a difference. Other times our service is distorted by our own rage and self-righteousness: "I know the way, and if you don't join my side you're wrong."

If all this weren't enough there are always the voices of ego. These trickster voices sound something like this to most of us: "Look how great I am. Look how politically correct I am. I am better and especially more spiritually evolved than you are. Wait until so and so hears what I am doing. I'm almost ready for full enlightenment!"

To unmask these shadow elements you need look at them openly and compassionately, remembering that we all get to observe the unhealthy parts of our ego when we serve others. Just as removing our personal mask is a central act of transformation, so too is removing the mask of our social self. I've found in my teaching that the simple act of bringing your shadow out into the light is enormously helpful; talk with others about your shadow material; find out what works in disarming it; even laugh about it. Too often we're afraid or embarrassed to admit our shadow, we keep it hidden, and that's when it has power over us.

The extraordinary thing is that service of any kind reveals the parts of you that still need healing. The shadows from your personal life follow you into the world, along with your skills for transforming them. All the core wounds from your life story will resurface, offering you an opportunity to grow in new and creative ways. As you care for others, you will find your personal healing is accelerated in ways you never imagined.

In tracing my own story, I identify with many of these shadow aspects. My service resume spans the last four decades like a historical overview of the major social trends in America. The 1960s found me tutoring children in the inner city and engaged in nonviolent resistance against the Vietnam War. In the 1970s I served in the Peace Corps, and was deeply involved with the Women's Movement.

The 1980s found me as a global peace activist and impassioned by citizen diplomacy in different hot spots in the world. As the 1990s arrived I threw myself into hospice work with people with AIDS and engaged in environmental sustainability work. Although it's embarrassing to admit now, I didn't really examine my deeper impulses around serving until the 1980's when I found myself utterly burned out.

I had just returned from Moscow where I had been training young Russian visionaries in the Empowerment model that my husband and I designed. I had worked rigorously for four days on concepts of self-responsibility, trust, self-esteem, sustaining hope, and creating concrete strategies to manifest these qualities. These were radical concepts in Russia at that time, and I was training over a hundred people virtually by myself. Because of the consecutive translation into Russian, the work required intense concentration during long twelve-hour days. It was exhilarating and exhausting work, for which I had donated my services and paid my own round-trip plane fare.

Several days after my return, a dear friend asked how my trip was. I began by saying "I didn't accomplish enough, there was so much more to do!" With strained urgency in my voice, I explained, "This is a window of opportunity where the new seeds of democracy can take hold. It won't last long—so I should really go back soon and do more."

My friend listened deeply to my story. When I was finished she asked, with great tenderness, "Why do you feel you can never do enough?" I began to cry. I realized at a core level, going back to the central image from my life story that I felt I would only be loved if I achieved more and more. In that moment I saw my secret desire for power and status. I heard the long litany of shoulds that often propelled my activism. Knowing my Joan of Arc complex, my friend compassionately and incisively reminded me, "You do not have to be a martyr in order to be effective." She helped me see I was burned out, that I had lost the original joy that inspired my work. She pointed out my spiritual arrogance—feelings of superiority because I did more than others, and my belief that if I didn't return to Russia the work would somehow stop without me.

After this difficult and important revelation, I worked with a spiritual counselor who helped me carefully examine my motivation to serve. I had to face parts of myself that I might have hidden or ignored without the catalyst offered by service. My work in the world was deepening my inner awareness. I was fine tuning my own rhythm of compassion, learning when to be on the in-breath, and when to be back out in the world.

It's helpful to have a trusted friend, colleague, counselor, or support group who can help you stay clear about your motivation to serve others. Someone like my dear friend who will tell you when you're burned out, arrogant, or caught up in a martyr syndrome. The next journal entry illuminates other ways the social shadow plays out. Linda reveals the mask of her perfectionism and the voices of her ego. Linda has been involved as a hospital volunteer for many years. Here, she describes what she learned about her motives as she tended her friend Rick.

This past summer as I supported my friend Rick as he died of cancer, I saw how big the "me" often is. Although I can be a genuinely compassionate and loving person, I finally realized that I have also gotten off on playing the role of "the conscious person." Now I have uncovered my narcissistic game and it's humiliating and shattering. In the guise of chasing the human potential and consciousness movement, I have often deluded myself. My new age resume reads long, impressive, and superficial.

So much of my desire to learn has really been my perfection-oriented ego. Though I've tried to suppress it, often when I serve I am more concerned about how well I am doing rather than being fully present. Being with Rick as he died, I realized that my search for consciousness has been, in part, a means to get ahead of my "not so conscious" family and friends. After all if I am more enlightened, then I am ahead in the pecking order.

Linda has so much courage to reveal the underbelly of her motivations. Underneath her mask of superiority was a great need to be accepted by friends and family, as well as her God. Remember that a mask produces the exact opposite of what it's intended for. Her perfectionism separated her both from those she hoped to serve as well as her loved ones. As she shatters her mask she feels deep humility. It's this vulnerable humility, as we will discuss shortly, that can help heal a shadow and allow us to connect deeply with others.

Often our social shadows signal deeper feelings of hopelessness or despair. This is so important because if unaddressed this kind of shadow leads to apathy and indifference. Part of my shadow includes feeling arrogant because I live more sustainably than others. In peeling deeper layers away I recognized arrogance was only the first layer. Under arrogance I found my despair that it's already too late to reverse the damage we've inflicted on the earth. Once I acknowledged my despair it didn't have so much power over me. Now I find that if I respect both my occasional feelings of despair along with my dedication to sustainability I am in truth with myself and inspired to act.

Some years ago I worked with a student named Bob who was gifted environmentalist. Bob knew more about sustainable living than most of us ever will. But he didn't walk his talk very well. As we explored the contradiction between what he knew and how he lived, Bob uncovered a deep seated belief that no matter how hard he worked for the environment it wouldn't matter. He was just one person and there would never be enough caring people to tip the balance. Bob's hopelessness showed up in the way he lived. Along with hopelessness he found rage and profound sadness.

Bob's story reminds us that intellectual knowledge doesn't automatically translate into compassionate action. Without the inner awareness of his shadow Bob's actions were empty and hopeless. As he came to understand and respect his shadow Bob could begin to heal his split, and walk his talk. He also began to help other environmental activists bring to the surface their hidden shadows as a means to continue their important work, preventing burnout and cynicism.

As we dig even further into the territory of our shadow, we begin to uncover the broad existential dilemmas that confront anyone who enters the heart of human suffering: despair and meaning; helplessness and effectiveness; action and reflection. As the visionary Executive Director of an AIDS service program Diane deals with these questions everyday. For several years she has led HIV Empowerment Support Groups, yet sometimes even she feels her efforts are inadequate.

As I look around the room at this HIV-support group, I feel a presence that we rarely acknowledge as we bravely keep up the good front. It's the undertone of constant sorrow. Eric is leaving and that is sad for all of us, then there are the deaths we will experience over the next months. Any variation in health of a group member is cause for concern, if not alarm. Each member of our group sees the future in the person sitting next to him.

They try to not let HIV define who they are but sometimes, as with any other positive group, this is impossible. They have more optimism than I do. They bravely work on their healing, and areas for change in their lives. They never suggest they won't be alive for the changes they are working towards. Sometimes I feel their lives are wasted. Lives that were difficult to begin with and won't get what they deserve this time around. What are they here to teach us?

So often I feel helpless to really understand or help. I feel like an observer offering minor assistance. I try to imagine what I would do if the shoe were on the other foot. But I can't do it! This is so frustrating; it makes me wonder who I think I am and what I think I'm doing. When I'm down in the pit of despair one of them says something that pulls me right back out. I like being here, I enjoy their company so much. Maybe that's enough, but I have a hard time believing this. I feel the need to do something, anything. Just sitting or witnessing doesn't seem sufficient.

I continue to struggle with the balance between action and simple presence. I feel resigned as it becomes obvious that I have no control over any of this. I worry about being too detached. Then I worry that I'm too caught up in the analysis of my service instead of the lives of these people I care so much about. It all seems less clear than it did a year ago.

One thing, however, is clear. I have not been able to help others as much as I thought I should. I have had to learn that my wishes for another's happiness are not enough to make them happy.

Confronting our social shadow is no easier than the work we did to uncover the hidden mask in our personal story. And it's no less important. The honesty of Diane's journal entry is moving. Here's a person who has made an enormous commitment to help ease the suffering in our world. Yet she wonders, does it matter? Can I ever do enough? These are questions that the small mind of the ego asks. As long as we remain in the limited boundaries of our ego we will never resolve these questions. Yet these very questions driven by the shadow of the ego can open the door to mature compassion.

Exercise: Uncovering Your Social Shadow

Close your eyes, quiet your mind, and gently follow your breath until you begin to relax.

In digging for your personal story you saw that it was essential to face the shadow of your central image and your false mask in order to find true self-understanding. Go back to your soul dig and review the work you did to expose your shadow.

Look deeply inside yourself and ask, What motivates me to serve? At first you will come up with all the positive reasons. Dig deeper and find the shadow of your motivation: power, status, approval, looking better than others, reaching enlightenment, perfectionism, guilt, or shame. Are you using addiction to service as an excuse not to do your own inner work? Are you motivated by rage or self-righteousness, or fueled by despair or indifference? Do you want to play God by controlling people or situations? Remember your shadow is mixed in with your genuine desire to care, and though it's embarrassing to admit, we all have shadow material. Take time to reflect, draw, and journal.

Now bring your shadow fully into the light. Write it down, draw what it looks like, say it out loud to yourself. Make a commitment to choose a trusted colleague, friend, or support group who you can talk to about your shadow. Consider whether you might need the help of a counselor or mentor to transform your shadow. For most of us transforming our shadow requires the reflection of someone else to help us face well-hidden parts of ourselves we'd rather not admit. Most important, keep bringing it out into the light, don't keep it hidden—that's when your shadow has power over you. And remember, be patient and compassionate with yourself. When you have finished this exercise take some time to read it over and reflect on your answers.

Eight

CULTIVATING A QUIET MIND
AND AN OPEN HEART

It is compassion that removes the heavy bar, opens the door
to freedom, makes the narrow heart as wide as the world.
Compassion takes away from the heart the inert weight, the
paralyzing heaviness; it gives wings to those who cling to the
lowlands of self.

—Nyanaponika Thera

Our shadows are the very teachers we need to find our way
to genuine service. They teach everything we need to know
about what doesn't work. The moral prescription of our
shoulds, our do-goodism, and our ideas of getting to heaven
destroys authentic caring. No matter how much service we're
engaged in, if it involves playing God or spiritual arrogance,
it's going to leave us empty and disillusioned. Martyr com-
plexes, fear, despair, or overanalysis of our skills reinforce the
illusion that we are either better than those we serve, or not
good enough. Either way this separation increases the suffering of those we hope to help, and more insidiously, it also
increases our own pain. We cannot fix or control suffering.
Nor can we make it go away with all our best intentions.

Whether you're a parent, therapist, business person, or activist—if your caring is motivated by any of these shadows—sooner or later you'll feel impotent and out of control. At some point you'll feel overwhelmed by the immensity of suffering and conclude that you're living in a senseless universe. Then your heart starts to close and your well of compassion begins to dry up. Paradoxically this very feeling of helplessness can catalyze a breakthrough in the way you respond to suffering.

After we pass through the romance phase of service, we enter the stage where we confront our shadows. Our shadows direct us to a deeper inquiry about the nature of suffering and we ask, as Diane did, how can I ever do enough, and does it matter anyway? We struggle to answer these questions with our rational mind, and we discover that we can't. Now we're ready to enter the third phase of excavating for the awakened heart where we learn to cultivate certain qualities that burst beyond the boundaries of the ego and lead us to genuine compassion. This phase can be compared to digging for the gifts from your parents and your place of belonging in your personal story. In both the personal and the social story, it is at this stage we uncover the qualities that offer the strength and courage to help us mature.

In the next two chapters we'll unearth the four qualities of mature compassion—a quiet mind, an open heart, loving presence, and radical simplicity—that allow us to move through the limitations of our shadow to a place of effortless generosity where serving flows naturally and freely. These qualities empower us to serve skillfully, drawing upon a source far greater than our ego. They expand the boundaries of our hearts beyond simplistic right and wrong positions. As the Buddhist teacher, Nyanaponila Thera, so beautifully reminds us, it is this mature compassion that "removes the heavy bar, opens the door to freedom, makes the narrow heart as wide as the world."

In chapter four, we met Sonya who designed a school serving the children and families in the inner city of Washington, D.C. The following entry from Sonya's service journal illuminates the continuing evolution of her rhythm of compassion. Here we witness her movement from service driven by her shadow into the first quality of mature compassion—a quiet mind.

When I first started working in the inner-city schools, I wanted to solve all the problems immediately. Things were not OK, and I was responsible to make them better. I put in incredibly long hours and rarely considered my own self-care. I was taking care of their lives, but I didn't have a life of my own.

One week there was a big crisis: three of our parents were put in jail. There was chaos at the school and everyone was overwhelmed. I went into overdrive and ended up getting really sick. While I lay in bed, I did some deep soul searching. Since I had a lot of quiet time to myself, I saw things more clearly. I realized the children and families in inner-city Washington, D.C., were on a journey. It wasn't my role to change them, fix them, or save them. I was on the journey with them, and this work was my healing process too.

After this, some things shifted. I started taking better care of myself by deepening my spiritual practice and getting enough rest. I found I was clearer and more peaceful when I was at school. The fruits of my quiet mind resulted in a subtle yet significant integration. I could feel that everything was OK, while at the same time, feeling the need for change. My capacity to hold these opposites, both acceptance and a passion to change things, has helped me to sustain my work and avoid burnout.

To be kind to another, I need to be kind to myself. Here's that gentle truth again. Yet, this is so deceptively simple many of us just don't heed it. Consequently we find ourselves overextended or burned out. Sonya's story is the classic scenario of the impassioned activist. She burned out, and then during her time on the in-breath something simple and profound took place. She quieted her mind and things became much clearer.

As she deepened her spiritual practice, Sonya was learning what the beloved meditation teacher, Thich Nhat Hanh tells us in *Being Peace* about stilling our minds: "Meditation is not a drug to make us oblivious to our real problems. Looking deeply at our own mind and our own life, we begin to see what to do and what not to do to bring about real peace in ourselves and in society." Like a still lake, the quiet mind allows us to see deeper than the surface mind of the ego. It softens the edges of the ego and helps us let go of the need to control, fix, or separate from suffering. It is spacious enough to gently hold the complex contradiction of acceptance and engagement that the rational mind can never reconcile.

Sonya's quiet mind, developed through her spiritual practice, allows her to understand two essential aspects of conscious service: we can't "save" or fix people, and our work to help others is just as much about our own healing as it is about theirs. Whether we're parenting, managing, mentoring, or healing people—as long as we engage with the surface mind of our ego we stay stuck needing to save them, to fix their suffering, or to try desperately to control situations.

All of these efforts are poignant and futile attempts to separate us from the inevitability of suffering—our own and our families, our friends and colleagues, our communities, and our world. The cultivation of a spacious quiet mind is essential in freeing ourselves from the tight boundaries of control and separation. It is the first step towards mature compassion and the doorway into the open heart, presence, and radical simplicity. And it provides the fertile ground for these other qualities to fully blossom.

THE QUIET MIND AS DOORWAY
TO THE OPEN HEART

To open deeply, as genuine spiritual life requires, we need
tremendous courage and strength, a kind of warrior spirit.
But the place of this warrior strength is in the heart.

—Jack Kornfield, from A Path with Heart

We've seen how the ego wants to fix, to make things perfect,
to reorder someone else's life, and above all, to do something
to maintain the illusion of control. We've also seen that in
order to grow in our capacity to care for others, a completely
different response is required. As Sonya learned, we need to
take time to sit still, quiet the mind, and listen deeply. In
Gandhi's words, "action without contemplation is blind."
Stories abound of his stubborn refusal to take action until he
was still and clear inside. Surrounded by crisis and chaos, he
would sit quietly spinning cotton. He was a living example of
the partnership of reflection and action. His example once
again reminds us to harmonize the in-breath and the out-
breath, literally as we quiet our minds and metaphorically as
we seek to balance action with contemplation as we serve.

My students and I heeded Gandhi's words and entered
concentrated periods of silence to clarify our vision of service. In the infinite container of the silence we reconnected
with the lessons from our life stories and with our primal
longing to connect with the human family. In the quiet of our
spiritual practice we found not a trace of should, guilt, or do-
goodism, but rather vast reservoirs of loving kindness waiting
to be utilized. Stillness was opening the door to our hearts.

As silence deepens, our minds become still and the voice
of the ego diminishes. Now we begin to hear the voice of the
heart. The heart is responsive to suffering without trying to

"fix it." The heart whispers all suffering is the same—yours, mine, society's, and the earth's—there is no use trying to separate yourself. The heart reminds us that we find freedom if we can enter fully into life and accept its great ocean of suffering. As we quiet the mind, the gentle voice of our heart speaks of a radical courage just waiting to be born.

As we delve further into the nature of mature compassion we see now that there are two equal partners working together—the still mind and the open heart. The still mind creates a quiet core from which we connect to the openness of the heart. In their partnership, they create a unity large enough to reconcile opposites and go beyond simplistic "either or" thinking. There is room for hope and despair, acceptance and engagement, and joy and suffering. Together a still mind and an open heart have the potent capacity to override the false chatter of our ego.

I had an experience that clearly illustrates the power of stilling the mind and opening the heart as a pathway to compassion. For many years I have had a love affair with China and her people. To experience this ancient culture so opposite from my own, to be in a place where a fifth of the human family resides, is simply intoxicating for me. Over the last decade I've been to China eight or nine times. During most my trips I traveled as a citizen diplomat, developing friendship and understanding between our cultures.

In 1989, I was planning a citizen diplomacy trip to China with a delegation of twenty-five people. On June 4th, we heard the devastating news of the Tiananmen Square massacre. As I listened to my car radio, I felt as if I had been violently punched in the stomach. I was so sickened by grief, confusion, and rage that I had to stop the car and throw up.

During the weeks that followed I faced an epic struggle—whether to go forward with my upcoming trip or stay home in protest. The vast majority of my colleagues advised me to cancel. People I held in the highest regard insisted that the journey would be dangerous and a terrible blunder politically, a sure statement that I supported the Chinese government. Others played to my Joan of Arc complex saying that I would be a heroine if I went forward and reached out to the people. I was in the middle of a storm with vehement opinions swirling in all directions.

For weeks I was a wreck, not knowing what to do. One day I took the afternoon off and went for a long hike in my beloved Catskill Mountains. As I hiked, my mind soon became still. I stopped near a brook and prayed for guidance. Things became very clear and simple. I saw the faces of my many Chinese friends. How could I close my heart and cut them off during a time of crisis? Could I only love China when times were open and she behaved "like America," and stay away when the going got tough? Part of the power of citizen diplomacy, as opposed to official diplomacy, was that we could still have contact with the Chinese people even though we thoroughly disagreed with the actions of their government.

On August 4th, exactly two months after Tiananmen Square, I left with twelve other citizen diplomats for China. We decided the main role of our trip was to act as witnesses, to listen with quiet minds and open hearts. We were the first unofficial Western delegation to have contact with the Chinese people since the massacre. The people with whom we met were overwhelmingly glad to see us.

During the trip we made a conscious effort to listen to diverse points of view with openness and equanimity. The Chinese people's reaction to Tiananmen Square was far more complex than the Western media reported. All, of course, deplored the bloodshed and hoped that calm would be restored. Some Chinese supported the students, but others felt they had pushed too far, or that they were intellectuals, out of touch with the majority of the Chinese people. Our quiet minds were capable of holding all of these opinions rather than demanding simple right or wrong answers.

We were able to hold the tension of the opposites: to acknowledge the government's position that it had acted legitimately in quelling violent turmoil, and the student leaders' belief that what happened was brutal repression of a peaceful reformist movement. Most importantly my heart's instinct that it was right to reach out in a time of crisis had been confirmed.

THE EARTH AS TEACHER OF STILLNESS AND OPEN HEARTEDNESS

What can we do
but keep on breathing in and out,

modest and willing, and in our places?
Listen, listen, I'm forever saying,

*Listen to the river, to the hawk, to the hoof,
to the mockingbird, to the jack-in-the-pulpit—*
                              —*Mary Oliver, from "Stars"*

One of the most eloquent teachers of stillness and open heartedness is the earth. The presence of the natural world is gentle, silent, and open. To befriend a tree, a river, or a creature we need a quieter rhythm than we might use with our human friends. It was my time with the mountains and the stream that allowed my mind to quiet and my heart to open around my dilemma about returning to China in 1989.

The still silence of nature teaches the same potent lesson of embracing the duality of life as we learn in the silence of prayer or meditation. Nature holds the opposites—light and shadow, order and chaos, creation and destruction—in a completely nonjudgmental way. The earth offers a never-ending symphony of unity in duality if we are quiet enough to listen. As we become more still we are able to hear more deeply. Many of my students find their mindful encounters with the natural world just as helpful as formal spiritual practice in reconciling both personal contradictions as well as the myriad of dualities inherent in serving the world.

When we approach nature with a still, sensitive rhythm we are awarded with a startling generosity. The natural world offers its spiritual secrets without hesitation. Poet and ecologist Gary Snyder tells us "We and nature are companions, and although authoritative voices do not speak from clouds, a vast, subtle music surrounds us, accessible via clarity and serenity." I experienced this generosity of spirit from the dolphins.

For many years friends had encouraged me to experience these extraordinary creatures who some scientists believe have highly evolved brains and communication capacities. Some months after the completion of a massive world peace initiative I helped organize, I traveled with several of my dearest women friends to a place where we could swim in the wild with the dolphins. I was still recovering from the exhaustion of my three-year involvement with the global peace initiative and I was looking forward to this time away.

I had heard many healing stories about the dolphins. I had also heard about the famous Buddha nature of their eyes, and on meeting the dolphins I immediately lost myself gazing into these great pools of compassion. But I wasn't prepared for what happened next. As I entered the water for my third swim two dolphins began to play with me. They tossed me gently into the air, catching me over and over again, singing in my ear with their unique high-pitched sound. They sustained this playful contact for over a half an hour. I was amazed that such giant creatures could play with me so gently. At first, all I was aware of was the incredible sensuality of their silky touch and their jubilant contact. Later I realized they were clearly trying to communicate something to me.

I quieted my mind, opened my heart, and sent the thought that I was ready to hear their message. Ever so gently I sensed the communication: "Thank you for all your work for world peace, we appreciate it. But for God sake don't take yourself so seriously. You can enjoy yourself at the same time you're dedicated to changing the world." At this point their singing was especially raucous, and then they released me back into the water and swam away.

For several weeks after this encounter I found myself unusually emotional and every time I thought of my two dolphin playmates I would cry. Not only had they offered me invaluable counsel, I felt as if I had fallen in love with them, so full was our connection. Over the years my visceral memory of their presence has served as a reminder to balance dedication with sensual joy, the out-breath with the in-breath.

The earth teaches us to quiet our minds and open our hearts. It helps us understand there are no simplistic truths and that as we care for others—as parents, as teachers, as employers, or as volunteers—there will always be conflicting feelings within us, as well as contradictory duality around us. We need a still center to anchor us, to help us stay steady as we live between the opposites. And we need a still, strong core to keep us connected to our open hearts from which the true impulse to serve originates.

SPIRITUAL PRACTICE: CULTIVATING A QUIET MIND AND AN OPEN HEART

> The fruit of silence is prayer,
> The fruit of prayer is faith,
> The fruit of faith is love, and
> The fruit of love is silence.
> —*Mother Teresa*

The partnership of a quiet mind and an open heart are cultivated through dedicated spiritual practice. Contrary to the instant enlightenment theories of the current day, dedicated practice is a life-long endeavor, as is the blossoming of genuine mature compassion a life-long unfolding. I have always told my students that I am less concerned with which spiritual practice they choose, than that they find one that works and then truly stay with it—for the long haul.

I work with students devoted to diverse spiritual belief systems including Catholicism, Judaism, Buddhism, the Baptist faith, the Native American tradition, metaphysics, and those still searching for their cosmology. Accordingly, they use a broad range of practices all of which are effective in stilling the mind and opening the heart. My years of teaching have clearly shown me that different people respond to different disciplines. Some of my students will never have a dedicated meditation practice but they have given themselves fully to daily yoga or tai chi. Others find their spiritual center the moment they enter the natural world—walking, running, or hiking each morning in silence and solitude. For still others there is a love affair with prayer and sacred text that inspires the necessary dedication. Like myself, many of my students use a combination of these practices: prayer, meditation, spiritual text, and time in nature.

In the purest sense, a practice of any form is time for solitude and silence—both endangered species in our fast-paced, overstimulated culture. It is a time to reconnect with the spirit, quiet the mind, and open the heart. It is a sacred space where we extract ourselves from our everyday activity and once again see things in a clear and true way. We all know the real work of a spiritual practice is the practice part. Ideally practice daily, and if this isn't possible several times a week for at least a half an hour. Committing ourselves to ride through the inevitable periods of resistance, boredom, or indifference that come with every discipline requires the warrior's spirit. Nothing less than a fierce desire to awaken—a passion to move beyond the small mind of the ego and the shallow impulses of the shadow—is required for genuine practice. It's very simple, without regular dedication practice is not practice.

This is not a book specifically about spiritual practice; rather it hopes to show the importance of a disciplined practice in cultivating mature compassion for our families, our world, and ourselves. Without some form of spiritual discipline we're like a small boat without oars in the midst of a great, and often turbulent, sea. If you already have a spiritual discipline, treasure it like a beloved, nurture it through regular dedicated practice, and make a warrior's commitment to stay with it for life. If you haven't yet found your form make it the highest priority to do so. Find a teacher or mentor to help you get started. Realize this could be one of the most meaningful things you ever do for yourself and those around you.

The following exercise will help you cultivate a quiet mind and an open heart. To do this you will be asked to choose, or reaffirm, a spiritual practice.

Remember, if you are just starting out it's going to take some time to find the practice that suits you best. Use this exercise, and the subsequent ones dealing with spiritual practice, as a way to open your exploration and bring forward the questions you might ask a teacher or mentor. There is no rush or pressure here. The process of finding your spiritual practice is a rich, first step in a lifelong endeavor. You will return to your chosen practice at various times throughout the book. My hope is that by seeing the myriad of ways your practice can be helpful, you will be inspired to strengthen your commitment

Exercise: Quieting the Mind, Opening the Heart

Close your eyes, quiet your mind, and gently follow your breath until you begin to relax.

Connect with your yearning to move through the limitations of your shadow to a place where caring flows naturally and freely. Feel your longing to serve others skillfully, drawing on a source far greater than your ego.

To fulfill these longings and find mature compassion you need to cultivate a quiet mind and an open heart through some sort of regular time for solitude and silence, a time to reconnect with your spirit. This spiritual practice is a sacred space where you extract yourself from your everyday activity and once again see things in a clear and true way. If you already have a chosen practice, please skip to the next part of the exercise. If you are searching for an appropriate practice, take time with the following questions:

- How do I find my spiritual center?
- How do I most easily quiet myself, becoming empty and able to hear the voice of my heart? Is it some physical activity in the natural world? Is it sitting still meditating, following my breath?
- Do I find my center through prayer or reading spiritual texts? Yoga or tai chi? Music or poetry? Do I feel inspired to use a combination of these practices?
- Do I need a teacher, class, or support group to help me get started?

For now, I will ask you to choose a practice and make a commitment to doing it for at least half an hour several times a week.

Using whatever practice you have chosen—praying, walking in nature, meditating, etc.—take about twenty minutes now and quiet your mind. Empty yourself and find a peaceful place within yourself. After twenty minutes visualize your quiet mind like a still lake where you can see deeper than the surface mind of your ego. Feel the hard edges of your ego—the need to control, fix, or separate from suffering—gently softening and letting go. What does your quiet mind tell you about how to care for yourself and others?

Visualize your quiet mind as a doorway into your open heart. Place your hands on your heart and listen to its gentle voice. Can you hear your heart whisper all suffering is the same—yours, mine, society's, and the earth's—there is no use trying to separate yourself. Listen as your heart reminds you that you can find freedom if you enter fully into life and accept its great ocean of suffering. What else does your heart tell you about serving others?

Imagine your quiet mind and your open heart joining together as equal partners. Your still mind offers a quiet core from which you connect to your open heart. Become aware that together they create a spacious unity large enough for you to reconcile complex contradictions. Imagine yourself immersed in this spacious unity. Now experience yourself capable of holding these opposites: joy and sorrow, acceptance and engagement, hope and despair. What other contradictions do you want to reconcile? What else are you aware of in this place of spacious unity? Take time to reflect, draw, and journal.

When you have finished spend a few more minutes with your chosen practice. You can incorporate this exercise with your ongoing daily practice as a way to continue cultivating a quiet mind and an open heart.

Nine

CULTIVATING PRESENCE
AND RADICAL SIMPLICITY

> No matter the kind of service being rendered . . . the ultimate
> worth of the effort will depend a good deal on how a partic-
> ular person manages to connect with those others being in
> some way taught or healed or advised or assisted: the chem-
> istry of giving and receiving as it works back and forth
> between individuals in one or another situation.
> —*Robert Coles, from* The Call of Service

A quiet mind and an open heart have prepared the way for the
next two aspects of mature compassion—presence and radical
simplicity. These two sisters grow naturally from a quiet and
open spiritual center. When we begin to serve, we have already
seen that our need to fix often eclipses our ability to be present
for others. As we mature, this need to fix suffering is replaced
with a desire to simply be present for another. Much of presence is about listening. Listening with "big ears"—ears that
don't need to resolve, or solve, or fix anyone. This kind of deep
listening is based on acceptance: acceptance of people, creatures, or the environment as they are, acceptance that we can't
control or manipulate the way events will evolve.

Presence is also about a relationship between equals. I bring my own brokenness as well as my strengths to those I care for. I heal and I am healed by the relationship. This mutuality allows me to see a whole person, creature, or river rather than as something in need of fixing. It also allows me to embrace the fullness of my humanity as I serve; joy and sorrow, fear and openness, and boredom and engagement are all part of the journey.

Elaine is a business executive who volunteers with Roberta, an older woman suffering from dementia. This excerpt from Elaine's service journal describes the rich exchange that occurs when we are present in this way.

I began my relationship with Roberta concerned that my "performance" with caring and compassion may not be adequate. Could I do it right? I must study about caregiving and frontal-lobe dementia. Now, that sounds funny! These days, I simply look forward to seeing Roberta and spending time with her.

Our relationship requires only that I be present to her—to listen, to laugh together, to cry, and hold hands while we walk down the street. Whatever shows up in conversation is "right" for that moment. Whatever is said is honored. A genuineness and love is growing. I've learned I need to bring nothing but myself and the bonds are created. It isn't about doing, it's about being wholly and completely with the other person.

Roberta has helped me as much as I may have helped her. I no longer fear her dementia. I witness her intellect disappearing but her love and compassion remain. I have been so enriched by our relationship.

Elaine describes what every caregiver, every parent, and everyone in relationship goes through. At first we're concerned about performance; we're self-conscious and nervous about doing the right thing. Gradually as we relax and trust more, we see that what really works is just being ourselves. Here we are, human to human, laughing, crying, and loving; this is enough. In the poignancy of our human condition we connect, and now we both give and receive. With mutuality there is more joy and less effort, a sure sign presence is emerging.

To deepen presence we sometimes have to face aspects of suffering that frighten or repulse us. We care for an aging parent who loses bodily functions, or a loved one with cancer suddenly doesn't recognize us. We volunteer to clean and tend oil-covered birds after an oil spill. In these instances remembering that we can't control things and remembering to simply be ourselves is especially helpful. Here we learn from Brenda who has been a hospice worker instrumental in developing a hospice program for children in her community.

I had often passed Mike in the hall on my other hospice visits and felt repulsed by him, hoping not to have any direct contact. His appearance was haunting and grotesque. He was in the terminal phase of AIDS and often he was in agony. While waiting for his next numbing medication, he would place a clip on his index finger and pinch it hard to divert his attention from the pain that was consuming him.

One afternoon I was cooking and serving meals, and every time I'd turn around there was Mike right beside me. As he stood near me I felt my life energy being pulled from my body—it was as if something was flowing out of me and into him. I did not experience this as draining in any way. In fact, I felt overcome with a sense of gratitude. It was like being with a young child whose needs were very pure. As if his illness had burned away the adult and left him with a tender vulnerability. I felt a deep connection and compassion for him. By my next hospice visit Mike had died.

We really witness Brenda's humanity here. Mike's intense suffering frightens and repulses her. It reminds her of her own suffering and that she too will die one day. We're all afraid of these things. And when we're afraid we separate ourselves from those in pain, hoping to avoid the reminder of our own impermanence. But Mike isn't afraid and he moves close to Brenda, offering her an opportunity to deepen in compassion. He is the teacher and in a certain way he is also the healer at that moment. In their experience we see how true service is a mutual exchange.

We learn from these journal entries that presence is the opposite of resolving or fixing. We felt presence when Elaine and Brenda were natural: listening, laughing, crying, cooking, or holding hands. Spontaneity replaced self-consciousness and made room for the grace of healing. Acceptance replaced the need to change or control suffering. Ultimately we understand that the exchange of our very humanness heals us and those we serve.

THE EARTH AS TEACHER OF MUTUAL PRESENCE

Each landscape asks the same question, I am watching myself in you, are you watching yourself in me.

—*Laurence Durrell*

At the very core of presence is the understanding of our mutual connection. Elaine and Brenda's presence evolved as they allowed the mutuality of their human condition to inform the healing process. This mutuality is equally important in caring for our nonhuman cousins. Just as this feeling of interconnection deepens our compassion for other people, reciprocity also strengthens our caring for the earth. And the earth itself is the great teacher of mutual interconnection.

Long before the scientific worldview convinced us otherwise, our ancestors worked with myth and ritual to portray the mutual interdependence of all life. They assumed a reality in which animals, plants, and inanimate nature were all mutually interactive with people. We don't just feel the wind, the wind feels us. Their stories and ceremonies revealed a profound respect for every form of life and a humble awareness of the human place in the larger web of existence.

At the conclusion of my Peace Corps service in West Africa I crossed the Sahara Desert. During this time I spent several weeks with the nomadic people known as the Tauregs, or the blue people because of the stark indigo blue of their desert garb. One day I learned that we would need to pack up camp and move by camel to another location. When I asked why the sudden need to move I was told a serious sandstorm was about five days away. I asked how they knew the sandstorm was coming and they said they could feel it, and some could also smell it. Later my guide and translator told me that the sandstorm itself had sent a communication to let them know to move their camps.

These gentle people regarded this reciprocity as an inherent part of their daily existence. At night, under the vast Sahara sky the Tauregs offered song and dance as a way to honor the web of life that sustained them. Their music was full of images that recognized the profound continuity between the sky, the stars, the desert, the camels, and themselves.

It is the recognition of this intrinsic interconnectedness of all life that needs to inform our caring for each other and the earth. When we feel this reciprocity deep in our hearts, a presence combining profound respect and mutual exchange surrounds our service.

THE RADICAL SIMPLICITY OF TRUE SERVICE

Almost anything you do will seem insignificant, but it is very important that you do it. You must be the change you wish to see in the world.

—*Mahatma Gandhi, from* The Political Philosophy of Mahatma Gandhi

As we learn presence it begins to teach us about its close sister—radical simplicity. The ego would like our service to be grand and heroic. It is often looking for power, acknowledgment, or a guarantee of spiritual brownie points. Authentic skillful service is far simpler. The ego steps aside and humility comes forward. Mother Teresa was a shining example of radical simplicity who helps us understand this component of mature compassion when she said, "One cannot do great things, one can only do small things with great love."

When I began my hospice volunteer work, my Joan of Arc complex was in full swing. I wanted to be heroic and bring all my great healing skills to my hospice clients. I soon learned that being with the dying was indeed heroic, but for completely different reasons than my ego conjured up. It was my hospice clients and their families who were brave. And it was they who ultimately healed me, allowing me to face my long, repressed grief over my mother's early death. My hospice work was a wonderful teacher about how simple genuine service really is—as this excerpt from my journal indicates:

Diana, the volunteer coordinator, has a new client for me. Larry is forty and in the final stages of AIDS. He contracted AIDS from his ex-wife. But before he knew that he was HIV-positive he had remarried Irene.

As I enter their home, Larry is lying downstairs, his breathing labored. I introduce myself, and Irene matter-of-factly takes me through a long list of errands that need to be done. She is clear, organized, and very much in control.

I am off to the bank, the drugstore, pet store, hardware store, post office and so on. This is not grandiose; it's just what needs to be done. When I get back to the house Irene is a very different person than the one I left several hours ago. I ask, "How are you doing?" and she starts to sob. I feel my heart break as I listen deeply to her sorrow. Her words tumble out. "It all happened so fast, he doesn't even know me anymore. His mom came yesterday and sat with him, and finally stopped denying that he was dying. I think that's part of the reason he is ready."

We talk for a long time about Larry, about life and death, about AIDS. I notice how beautiful Irene's eyes are. I am deeply moved by her courage in facing her husband's death. I feel blessed to be in her presence. This is probably the only encounter we will ever have, and we have already exchanged everything important. As we unload the groceries, Irene is pleased with the special birdseed I got. She says how wonderful that the birds will have treats and that life will go on.

Soon it's time to go. We embrace, and I tell her my prayers are with her. I say good-bye to Larry whom I have never met, but in some mysterious way I feel I've known for a long time.

As I drive home it seems the mountains have never been so lovely, the sunset so soft and comforting. I phone my husband, David, the moment I arrive to tell him how much I love him. The next morning Hospice calls to tell me that Larry has died peacefully.

As my heart opens more, I am immersed in the mystery of life. It is immense and surprising. It is both cruel and kind. I have moments of understanding and many moments when I feel lost. Yet I am learning that regardless of what I am feeling, service is actually radically simple. It is doing what needs to be done in the moment with a loving heart. In the enormity of life's suffering I am both big and small. I can't end the suffering, but I can encounter it with greater and greater compassion. I am learning what a privilege it is to be alive and on this journey of awakening.

Radical simplicity gently demands that the ego step aside so we can encounter suffering with equanimity. In this state, we neither run away from pain nor overdramatize it. We live with divine insecurity, having little control over the people or situations we serve. Gradually we discover the small ego self is being replaced by a startling largesse combining acceptance, presence, and humility. In her book, *Holy Daring*, Carmelite Mother Tessa Bielecki says this about the humility inherent in radical simplicity: "To be humble is to walk in truth—the truth of who we are and who God is. Since humility is truth, it does not mean thinking little of ourselves, but thinking of ourselves very little. This virtue is not for wimps but for warriors! Humility carries with it a breadth of greatness, a jubilant freedom, and holy audacity. . . ."

An entry from Steve's journal demonstrates this broadening of the human spirit, this holy daring. Steve is a businessman who works in his family's company. As a volunteer, he has a particular love for the elderly.

I cannot pretend that the pain of suffering doesn't get to me, it does. I practice being quiet every day so that I can go inside when I feel overwhelmed. Then I simply ask, what can I do to serve? And I simply take the next step, knowing that this is enough. I am content to be one part of the solution and know that I cannot fix it all. I am growing more and more comfortable with not knowing and being able to serve from a place of oneness and compassion.

The most important thing I can do is be present to suffering in its many forms. Be present and recognize that suffering exists everywhere, all the time. I know that I am only part of the solution—and I know now that this is enough.

Like all of us, Steve eventually realized that it's impossible to understand suffering intellectually—it's just too big and unfathomable for the mind. But it is possible to embrace it with the heart. Steve didn't demand rational answers; rather he found the peace of simply being present was enough.

Exercise: Cultivating Presence and Radical Simplicity

Take a few minutes to quiet your mind and open your heart. Become aware that your quiet mind and open heart have prepared the way for the next two aspects of mature compassion—presence and radical simplicity. These two sisters of compassion lead you into the very essence of your humanity.

Recall a situation where you were caring for someone, or for some part of the natural world, who was suffering—a sick child or parent, a client or colleague in pain, a stranger in need, a wounded animal, a polluted river, or a dying forest. Become aware of your initial feelings—maybe you were concerned about performance, self-conscious or nervous about doing the right thing, wanting to fix or control the situation. Your ego wants your service to be grand and heroic. It's looking for power or a guarantee of spiritual brownie points. Just let yourself feel these impulses, no need to hide them; we all have them. What else do you feel at this initial stage of caring? Take time to reflect, draw, and journal.

Staying with the same situation, once again quiet your mind and open your heart. Imagine that all you have to do is be fully present to the person or creature in your care; all that's required to serve skillfully is radical simplicity. Feel the relief in this; no need to perform or do "the right thing"; no need to run away from their pain or overdramatize it. Now visualize yourself listening deeply to this person or creature's pain. See yourself accepting things as they are without needing to change or control anything. Ask what is needed in this moment, and visualize yourself doing it with a loving heart.

Now you begin to see that this simple, humble presence is really about being yourself. What qualities help you to just be yourself when you care for others? Consider the gifts from your parents and your sense of belonging from your personal story as some of the qualities that allow you to relax and be natural. What happens when you let go of self-consciousness and just be yourself? Take time to reflect, draw, and journal.

Imagine feeling more and more at ease just being yourself: listening, laughing, crying, and caring. Consider how this exchange of your very humanness is healing both you and the one in your care. Can you feel yourself being healed by the one you are caring for? How do you experience this mutuality that allows genuine caring to take place? Take time to reflect, draw, and journal.

When you finish take some time to read over your journal. The next time you find yourself caring for a family member, a colleague, a friend, a client, or a nonhuman friend, come back to this exercise to help you stay centered. And remember that presence asks that you simply be yourself and humbly do what's needed with a loving heart.

From Moral Obligation to Effortless Generosity

The migrating bird leaves no trace behind and does not
need a guide.

—Dogen, from "Coming or Going"

With time and practice this quartet of soulful qualities—a
quiet mind and open heart, presence and radical simplicity—
begin to blend and sing as one. When this happens, we arrive
at a state of effortless generosity. A desire to serve and contribute that is so natural, so joyful that it simply overflows
from us. Like a ripe fruit tree we effortlessly offer our generosity. This mature generosity is traceless and leaves little
room for the ego. We engage deeply but without concern for
moral obligation, do-goodism, or grandiosity.

Conscious caring takes practice. Kathie is a teacher, poet,
and grandmother who volunteers with Rose, an elderly woman
living with her children. Kathie's journal entry offers a lovely
summary of the stages we pass through on the way to mature
caring. First, we see her awkwardness, full of ego concerns; gradually she begins to relax and be herself, and openness, presence,
and simplicity evolve; finally we witness joy and spontaneity as
she and Rose connect at the core of their human condition.

When I first started with Rose, my fears and lack of self-confidence kept
me on the edge of things rather than at the heart of them. I often sat in
the living room while Rose slept in the bedroom. I didn't really understand my mission. Then later I began to sit and watch TV soaps with her,
and she began napping on the living room couch to be among the living. We shared spaces, and we shared the silent resting time too.

Now I see my contribution more clearly and more simply. I was
there to give Rose's son assurance that he could go to work and

know that Rose was safe. I discovered I was a source of comfort to Rose early on when she said, "I always feel well cared for when you are here." Over time I was able to flow with her energetic moods, with her criticisms, with drug-inspired psychotic bouts, with her tiredness, and spaciness.

Gradually we began to play more, taking five-minute adventure walks up the block, enjoying a well-cooked omelet together. I was here to co-create some comfort, security, and pleasure in both our lives. I was here to be disappointed when things didn't go as I thought they should, and to observe that that is part of the learning, too. I was here to learn, step-by-step, what it means to be compassionate.

Ultimately service teaches us about conscious living and gives us the skills any parent, spouse, boss, manager, caretaker, or volunteer needs in order to become a more compassionate person. Like Kathie, we all need to acknowledge the shadow impulses of our caring, and find our rhythm of compassion. A quiet mind and an open heart are the fruits of our practice—as is the understanding that we are healed by those we care for.

As the Dalai Lama said, "The realization that we are all basically the same human beings, who seek happiness and try to avoid suffering, is very helpful in developing a sense of brotherhood and sisterhood, a warm feeling of love and compassion for others." This intimacy with all living things is at the heart of effortless generosity, as it shatters the illusion that we are separate and inspires us to care for one another.

The Indian sage, Rabindranath Tagore, said at the end of his life: "I slept and dreamt that life was joy, I woke and found that life was service, I acted and behold service was joy." A passage from Sonya's journal illustrates this wisdom and concludes this chapter.

Tyrell is four years old, with a mother on crack and a father in jail, and a neighbor is raising him. Three weeks ago his natural mother kidnaped him. We didn't know if we were ever going to see him again. But the police found him and returned him to his guardian. He epitomizes the violence that the children I work with have to endure. Tyrell taught me more than my little heart could hold—my heart had to grow.

But Tyrell also taught me not to keep him in a box called suffering, because he also teaches me about joy and resilience. For two years he never talked at school. But now he talks to me constantly. I would even call him a motor mouth. I just learned that Tyrell adores riding his bike. It's blue with stickers on it and he keeps it at his grandmother's house. All those stories and questions he held in for so long are pouring out of him.

Exercise: Arriving at Effortless Generosity

Using your chosen spiritual practice, take about fifteen minutes to empty and find a peaceful place within yourself. Now imagine the four qualities of mature compassion—a quiet mind and open heart, presence and radical simplicity—as a quartet of qualities within you. Each quality has a beautiful tone and resonance.

First, hear the voice of your quiet mind reminding you that stillness allows you to go deeper than the surface mind of the ego, and helps you loosen the ego's tight boundaries of control and separation.

Now hear the gentle voice of your heart whisper: all suffering is the same, yours, mine, society's, and the earth's; there is no use trying to separate yourself.

And now the voice of your presence says there's no need to worry about performance or "doing the right thing": just be yourself, listen deeply, and remember caring is a mutual relationship.

Finally, you hear the voice of radical simplicity saying, just do whatever is needed in the moment with a loving heart. Take a few moments to really listen to each voice in the quartet.

Imagine these four voices—a quiet mind, an open heart, presence, and radical simplicity—blending and singing as one. What do you hear? Now bring to mind a human or non-human who is suffering. Visualize yourself caring for them with all of these qualities working in unison. What do you experience? Can you feel your natural desire to care, so spontaneous and so joyful it simply overflows from you? Bring Tagore's beautiful words into your heart, "I slept and dreamt that life was joy, I woke and found that life was service, I acted and behold service was joy." Take time to reflect, draw, and journal.

When you have finished this exercise make a commitment to spend time with the member of the human or earth family you have just focused on. Try to care for them with the four qualities of mature compassion working in unison. And remember compassion is a practice, it deepens with time and dedication.

Ten

SERVICE AS A
SPIRITUAL PRACTICE

If while we practice, we are not aware that the world is suffering, that children are dying of hunger, that social injustice
is going on a little bit everywhere, we are not practicing
mindfulness. We are just trying to escape.
   —*Thich Nhat Hanh, from* Living Buddha, Living Christ

As we uncovered our personal story in Part I there came a
point when our story was full and mature enough that we
could face the challenge of heartbreak and radical surprise. At
that juncture we had the confidence to encounter our suffering at deeper levels. We learned that the way we related to
our brokenness determined whether our heart awakened or
closed, and whether we could find meaning in our suffering
rather than give in to despair. We also learned that our very
brokenness was our connection to the unbroken whole.

   Now we have reached this same juncture in joining the
story of the world. Practicing the qualities of mature compassion we are ready to encounter the pain of the human family
and the earth family at more complex levels. Once again we
must walk into the fire of heartbreak as we engage with the

immensity of suffering. We now enter the final phase of excavation in digging for the awakened heart where we discover service and stewardship as extensions of spiritual practice.

Serving from a place of effortless generosity we experience intimacy with all living things and we are naturally moved to care for those who are in pain. In this mysterious intimacy we feel profoundly connected with strangers, people, and creatures we've never met. In this place of universal connection, service becomes part of our spiritual practice. The way we encounter our own and the world's suffering begins to change.

For service to become an extension of our spiritual practice we must learn to open to suffering, to feel it, connect with it, and let it flow through us. To fully engage with this process I ask my students to work with the mantra "my heart is breaking, my heart is awakening." This reminds us that each time our heart breaks it also grows stronger. Our compassion matures, and we're capable of seeing the true nature of suffering and responding skillfully to it.

This kind of heartbreak is not about collapse, despair, or overdramatization. As discussed in our personal story this heartbreak does not give in to the seduction of self-indulgence or the dead end of victimization. Rather it is born from passionate engagement with the world. At this phase in our caring our heart awakens. We find awe and gratitude for the mystery of life, a luminous knowledge of the self, and a growing desire to surrender to God. Our service becomes a part of our practice that renews and sustains us. It becomes our path to freedom.

In this divine irony, generosity leads to heartbreak, and heartbreak leads to liberation. The mystic, Simone Weil, put it this way when she spoke of the heart dying of sorrow, "We have to die in order to liberate a tied-up energy, in order to possess an energy which is free and capable of understanding the true relationship of things." Poets and mystics have long known that a savage awareness of suffering leads to intimacy, acceptance, and rare appreciation of the beauty of the world.

I am blessed to have felt this awe and intimacy with thousands of people all over the globe. In 1983, my husband, David, and I were deeply troubled by the Cold War, predictions of nuclear disaster, and the escalating arms race. The Soviet Union was the great enemy. To show our concern, we launched a grassroots initiative to demonstrate the world's desire for peace.

In 1980, David served as the director of the Olympic Torch Relay. Using his expertise he envisioned the First Earth Run. A torch of peace would be passed around the world to symbolize the human family's yearning to live in harmony. I joined him, and we spent the next three years of our lives organizing this initiative in cooperation with the United Nations Children's Fund (UNICEF). In 1986, the torch was passed through sixty-two countries. Twenty-five million people and forty-five heads of state participated in the event and the project raised several million dollars for the neediest children in the world.

By the end of this endeavor we were exhausted and totally broke, but we had experienced three of the most fulfilling years of our lives. I had quite literally met the human family during our epic journey. I was not new to the developing world, having worked in West Africa and South America, yet my heart broke many times as I witnessed the poverty in Africa, the over population and filth in India, the spiritual starvation in the Eastern Block, and the isolation in remote parts of Asia. But my heart also broke in another, unexpected way.

It broke open to receive this precious family of humanity. On a West African night a sea of ten thousand African faces illuminated by candles surrounded us. Hundreds of Chinese schoolgirls with bright pink bows tied in their hair taught us to play their own version of patty cake. The full moon lit our way as Indonesians carried the torch through Java to the mesmerizing sound of gamelan orchestras. In

Moscow, people reached out from the crowds to clasp our hands and touch the torch of peace as we journeyed through the snowy streets.

These faces have stayed with me through the years. They come to me in my dreams as if to say, remember us, we are part of your family; our joys and sorrows, our hopes and dreams are the same as yours. "We are the world" is not just a jaded slogan, it's a truth that needs to inspire our action and infuse our spiritual practice. The American astronauts were changed forever as they saw the earth from outer space. And I was changed forever as I met the human family during the Earth Run's eighty-six-day epic journey.

In our trainings, David and I have shown a video of this event to thousands of people throughout the world. A panorama of the earth's people—black, yellow, white, red, old, young, famous, unknown, rich, and poor demonstrate their yearning to live together as one human family. At the end of the video most people in the audience are weeping. They are feeling a connection so primal that many are unable to put their feelings into words.

As we mature in our service, this enigmatic intimacy with the human family propels our caring. We learn to let our hearts break open both to the depths of humanity's suffering and to the depths of its love.

SUFFERING IS UNIVERSAL

Suffering has a way of getting inside you. When you see the injustice that's causing the suffering you've got to do something about it. Otherwise you become complicit.

—Sister Helen Prejean, from Dead Man Walking

As we open more, our service becomes more like spiritual practice, and we start to see the unclouded truth: suffering is universal. We come to the overwhelming recognition that suffering is everywhere. In the faces of the people at the bank and the stores where we shop, the person who delivers our mail, in our families, our friends, and our own lives; in the raw pain of the homeless, and those on the margins of society.

In her book, *Lovingkindness: The Revolutionary Art of Happiness*, Sharon Salzberg says we can ease this suffering only when we accept the universal nature of it. "What a tremendous relief to have the actual truth openly spoken. 'There is suffering in this world.' Everything is up front. There are no games, no pretense, no denial. To acknowledge the truth of suffering allows us to feel our unity with others. The goal of our spiritual practice is to be able to understand, to be able to look without illusion at what is natural in this life, at what is actually happening for others and for ourselves. This willingness to see what is true is the first step in developing compassion."

Genuine acceptance of the world's pain is full of compassion and without rancor. Yet this kind of acceptance is never complacent. It is fiercely aware. By accepting the presence of suffering, we are also accepting responsibility for engaged action. The reconciliation of these opposites—acceptance and responsibility—is a true sign of spiritual progress. As the Buddha said, "I teach one thing and only one thing: that is, suffering and the end of suffering."

The following service journals show that we have a choice to either defend against the universality of suffering, or be open to it. Often our first response is to deny or run away from it. We harbor the illusion that we can avoid something that's simply everywhere. Steve candidly admits what everyone feels at some point in the journey:

I have built a big wall to protect myself from suffering because it just plain hurts too much. I run away from suffering, and it hurts to know that sometimes there is little I can do. At those times, I just feel guilty, and I have no self-worth. My mind is blown away by the amount of suffering people endure. I don't understand why there has to be so much, so I build my wall of protection higher.

Steve's last two lines are deeply human and deeply instructive. If we attempt to understand suffering with the intellect, we'll stay defended. Steve implies that if only he could understand suffering with his rational mind he could somehow eliminate it. Much like being able to fix a car engine once he knows how it works. Of course, we all know this isn't true—though at times we all desperately wish it were true. There is simply no way we're going to eradicate suffering. But what we can do is remove our barriers and defenses that we use to try to avoid pain.

To move through our defenses we return to quieting our minds and opening our hearts. More than ever we realize the essential role of our chosen practice as we turn to prayer, meditation, time in nature, or a long talk with a trusted friend or counselor to remind us that we can't fix suffering, but we can be present to it. We're reminded that in our suffering we're all the same. Then gently, our heart opens again. We will repeat this rhythm of opening and closing our hearts many times in our lives. This is the way we learn to be more compassionate to others and ourselves.

As the heart opens, we may confront vast and unexpected feelings, as did Diane, in her work as the executive director of an agency working with AIDS.

Fred walks into the conference room leaning on a cane and wearing dark glasses and a baseball hat. He is pale, haggard, and wasted with the unmistakable look of someone in the final stage of AIDS. The staff grows silent, unable to believe that this is the person they have known and worked with for the past five years.

I can just barely stand to look at him. I am so shocked by what I see. All our differences go out the window. I don't for one minute care how much trouble he has caused me, the agency, and the staff. It is impossible to think of things like that when confronted by this degree of suffering. You assume that when you reach this moment, you will be prepared. Bullshit. There's no way you are prepared to see a feisty, active thirty-year-old reduced to someone who will be lucky if he makes it for another month.

Who's suffering here? It seems that we all are. Staff members come up to me later to talk about their feelings, "He is clearly not doing well," "I feel like I was kicked in the stomach." What a lesson in the universality of suffering. Pain, helplessness, hopelessness, death, you name it, all rolled up into one not-so-tidy little ball.

Diane teaches us that we can't "prepare" for suffering; at some point each of us will be knocked over by the immensity of it all. Though she is shocked by Rick's pain, the beauty of Diane's response is that she doesn't defend; rather, she opens to the universality of suffering. There is absolutely no pretense in her reaction. It is stunning, raw, and true—a beautiful mess. She also teaches us that we can only face the universality of suffering by dealing with the particulars of it. Diane responds to the immediacy of Rick's pain—his haggard, wasted, dying body. This immediacy opens her heart and suddenly, what seemed important no longer matters. Then moving from the particular back to the universal Diane realizes everyone in this encounter is suffering.

There comes a time when all of us hit the wall and feel overwhelmed by the pain we encounter. This might come from an experience of loss, illness, divorce, or simply in the daily acts of caring for our families and friends. Judith is an artist, mother, and active person in her community. In this journal entry she describes a week of heartbreak and awakening.

Some days, I wondered whether Rita would live forever. I wondered, too, whether I could continue to endure the TV talk shows that blared on through my visits to the nursing home. Then on Friday morning, Rita died peacefully. Her daughter and I kept a vigil but no one notified her estranged sons. There was no moving reconciliation of this broken family. Still Rita left us in great peace, though down the hall a man wailed and cried out, begging death to spare him.

Thirty miles away, my friend Sylvia lies paralyzed, gazing at the ceiling. The other day, I stood helpless next to her bed, listening to the gurgle of her stomach tube. A recent stroke claimed her speech, as well as her left side. A few years ago, in a cruel victory, Sylvia had courageously trained herself to scrawl and limp when another stroke paralyzed her on the right. Now she has no body left.

Then there's Angela who left an abusive marriage last winter, three months pregnant. We agreed that I would be her partner-coach at the home birth. At the six-week Lamaze class we were an odd couple. "Don't touch me," she cautioned as the other beaming couples snuggled in to watch the videos. Physical contact stimulated too much terror.

This week—on July 26th at 4:25 A.M., exactly one year after my father's death—the phone rang. Angela was in active labor, I should come right away. Eager to facilitate the birth, I reminded her of her breathing exercises. I was stung when she snapped, "Shut up." I prayed in the silence by her bed and held her seven-year-old as the beautiful baby arrived pink and healthy.

I have learned that suffering is absolutely everywhere. The question is: can I stay open, can my humanity burst through, and remain green and fragrant in the midst of it?

How aware and how raw these entries are. You can feel the shock, helplessness, and confusion. Here we are, this is life, and we're right in the middle of it. There's no more thinking, "when this is over it's going to be different, there will be no more pain." Yet these passages also show the moving quest to accept the universality of suffering. Like Steve, Diane, and Judith, we must search within to find the resources we need to face the human condition. And to keep asking, how can we stay open?

Exercise: Staying Open: Service as Spiritual Practice

Return to your chosen practice for about fifteen minutes to quiet your mind and open your heart. Now take some time and experience your connection with the human family. Visualize the people in your family, in your community, and in different parts of the world. Gather them all around you. What do you feel as you look into these people's eyes? Take time to reflect, draw, and journal.

Along with your connection with the human family comes the awareness of its suffering. Take a few deep breaths and open your heart to feel the suffering that surrounds you. Visualize some specific moments of pain: first feel a specific moment of your own suffering; now feel the suffering of your family and friends; feel the suffering of your community, society, and the world at large. Become fully aware that your first response is to defend yourself against the pain; you try to deny or avoid it; you attempt to understand it with your intellect. Experience how your heart begins to close as you defend, deny, avoid, or rationalize the suffering around you. Just let yourself feel these things, they're completely natural and human. Take time to reflect, draw, or journal.

Now imagine your mind like a deep, still lake. Enter the depths of this stillness where there is no need to defend against pain, there is room for all of it. Listen to the voice of your heart as it gently reminds you there is no need to understand suffering, just open to it. Now breathe deeply, keep your heart open and say these phrases out loud several times:

- Suffering is everywhere.
- We all suffer.
- Pain will always be part of life.
- In our suffering we are all the same.

How does it feel to keep your heart open and simply acknowledge the universality of suffering? Most of us go through a wide mixture of responses from sadness, rage, despair, resignation, and then, relief, calm, and acceptance. Let yourself pass through the gamut of your feelings, the most important thing is to just stay open. Take time to reflect, draw, or journal.

Now bring the suffering of someone you know—a child or parent, a colleague, client, cherished pet or friend—into your heart. Again focus on some concrete aspect of their pain. Keeping your heart open, begin to follow your breath. On the in-breath take in their suffering with the wish that they be free of pain; on the out-breath send out love and healing. Breathe in their suffering with the wish that they be free of pain, and breathe out sending love and healing. Practice this for a few minutes. Now do the same thing for yourself, breathing in your suffering with the wish that you be free of pain, breathing out sending love and healing. What was your experience as you stayed open to the pain? What did you learn from this? Take time to reflect, draw, or journal.

This practice of breathing in suffering and breathing out love and healing is a Buddhist meditation called *tonglen*. It helps to use *tonglen* whenever you are facing pain. Try using this practice as you go through your day with your family, at work, hearing the news of the world's suffering. Practicing *tonglen* over time you will notice that you begin to stay more and more open.

Eleven

STEWARDSHIP AS
SPIRITUAL PRACTICE

For the moment all you have to know is that two fundamen-
tally different stories have been enacted here during the lifetime of man. One began to be enacted here some two or
three million years ago by the people we've agreed to call
Leavers and is still being enacted by them today, as success-
fully as ever. The other began to be enacted here some ten or
twelve thousand years ago by the people we've agreed to call
Takers, and is apparently about to end in catastrophe.

—Daniel Quinn, from Ishmael

In certain Eastern spiritual traditions the awakening of compassion for the human family instantly puts one on the path
of ecological compassion. But in the West, we have been far
slower to make this essential connection. We have become so
myopic in our obsession with personal healing that we've forgotten that our well-being is inseparable from the healing of
the planet. Today we have an urgent need for an ethics of
compassion that goes beyond human caring to include the
earth and all its nonhuman inhabitants.

Just as we explored service to the human family as an

extension of spiritual practice, so we too need to experience our stewardship of the earth as intrinsic to our practice. In this chapter we will explore two fundamental arenas that help us blend stewardship and spiritual practice: connecting the state of our soul with the state of the planet, and living sustainably as a pathway to mindfulness.

For many of us the first step toward stewardship as spiritual practice is the fundamental recognition as stated by James Hillman: "Psychology, so dedicated to awakening human consciousness, needs to wake up to one of the most ancient human truths: we cannot be studied or cured apart from the planet." In Hillman's statement we arrive at the heart of both our ecological and our moral crisis—our alienation from the whole that we're part of and our disconnection from our future. Two of the greatest forms of suffering in the Western world are our alienation from each other, and our alienation from the earth. Just as we seek to heal the alienation between individuals, families, and societies, we need to heal our alienation from the natural world.

Today there is so much talk of soul, and loss of soul. It is heartbreakingly clear that our loss of soul is, in part, a direct reflection of our desecration of the earth. The human family's spiritual bankruptcy is in direct proportion to our disregard for the planet we live on. As we destroy the earth we too are at risk of destroying some essential part of our humanity. Indeed the health of the planet and the health of the human psyche are a seamless continuum.

Paradoxically, for many of us it's our connection with the earth that reawakens our soul and imbues us with a sense of the sacred. Often some of our deepest personal healing takes place through our relationship with the natural world. But this subversive split—the desire to be healed by nature while we continue to harm it by living unsustainably—can never lead to genuine, whole healing. By joining sustainable living with spiritual practice we can mend this split, making the circle whole again—we heal the earth as the earth heals us.

My own story is illustrative of the gradual awakening many of us pass through in order to become more aware of how our unconscious overconsumption is affecting both our own spiritual health as well as the health of the planet.

For all my life I've felt reverence for the earth, but until recently I had given little thought to my responsibility to the planet or how my lifestyle might be destructive to the fragile balance of life that I am part of. Up until the late 1980s I was deeply involved with world peace, citizen diplomacy, and other social causes. Like most people when it came to the ecological crisis I took the out-of-sight out-of-mind path. I knew it was important to recycle and I got involved with Earth Day but these were isolated gestures that hadn't really taken root in my heart. Then I had a wake-up call. David and I were invited to play the World Game, a remarkable experience conceived by the visionary Buckminster Fuller.

Bucky's genius was to provide people with a visceral experience of the actual distribution of our planet's resources. The *World Game* was played on a gigantic world map laid out on a gymnasium floor. The players were divided across the map according to the actual population density of each continent. Flashlights were distributed to represent energy, loaves of bread for food, and jugs of water represented drinkable water.

I ended up in Africa, a continent I love and have lived in. We were jammed together on our portion of the globe with a few measly sticks of bread, very little water, and even fewer flashlights. The gym went dark and everyone was asked to turn on their flashlights–producing glaring light in the Northern Hemisphere and almost darkness in the

Southern Hemisphere. Then we held up our sticks of bread—the North covered with bobbing loaves of nourishment while the entire continents of India, Africa, and South America appeared to have less food than the East Coast of North America. And so it went with water.

Then we were asked to stand in silence and simply look around the room. Across the world I saw my homeland, the United States, full of space for people to stand, so much bread, water, and flashlights people could barely hold them all. Suddenly, the fact that we Americans are only a tiny five percent of the human family and yet we use an astonishing one third of our entire planet's resources, became heartbreakingly real for me. The longer I stood there the worse I felt—shame, injustice, rage, desire to run away, and finally deep sadness.

David and I returned home deeply affected by our experience. For weeks I struggled with the outrageous inequality between the North and South. Why did I get so lucky and how did I get so greedy? How should I live now that I understood the preposterous consumption and waste in the United States? Should I move back to Africa and try to help out? At the deepest level I was once again asking myself how can I find peace of mind when such suffering and inequality abound in our world? Thus began a new period of inner searching for a skillful response to the world situation.

In typical fashion, David's response was to plunge into the heart of the beast. He began to read everything available on the consumption patterns and habits in the United States. He talked to the experts and asked lots of questions. Our living room became a clearinghouse for the latest information on consumption, sustainability, and every sort of ecological dilemma. David's research made it abundantly clear that the consumption patterns of American households were a big part of the environmental crisis, and potentially a significant part of the solution. As the months passed he found ample statistics on the problems we faced but a shocking lack of information about what the average citizen could do in response to the immensity of the crisis.

This inspired him to found his organization the Global Action Plan for the Earth (GAP) dedicated to empowering citizens to create environmentally sustainable lifestyles in America and other high-consumption countries.

With my husband on the forefront of the sustainability movement, I had an amazing crash course on how to respond effectively to the ecological crisis. I realized I didn't need to move back to Africa to help out. Where I could help most was right here in America—the way we lived was a big part of the problem and changing our consumption habits in our homes and our communities could make a significant difference. I became David's "woman in the street" as he tested many of his ideas about sustainable living on me. When David created GAP's "Household EcoTeam Program"—the four-month program that actually teaches people how to make their homes earth friendly—we formed the first EcoTeam along with six of our friends. Since that first EcoTeam I've had the pleasure of coaching teams throughout the United States, helping people change their consumption patterns and create sustainable lifestyles.

Along with everything pragmatic I was learning about sustainability I became deeply interested in the spiritual dimension of stewardship. As I taught people about sustainable living it became increasingly clear to me that each earth-friendly act—composting, reusing, recycling, repairing, car pooling, eco-wise shopping, conserving water and energy—was also an act of ecological mindfulness. Sustainable living offered ongoing practice in mindfulness. I was learning that effective stewardship was a balance of reverence and responsibility.

I found many people were more motivated to maintain their sustainable habits when they were imbued with the context of spiritual practice. The stewardship ethic helped people simplify their lives reprioritizing what really mattered such as family, community, and time for long-forgotten dreams. As an antidote to the addiction of consumerism, stewardship could help heal the spiritual emptiness at the core of so many lives.

Slowly but surely I had connected my own story to the story of the earth, and now I was inspired to help others make this connection.

FINDING THE PERSONAL LINK

The problem, then, is how to bring about a striving for harmony with land among a people many of whom have forgotten there is any such thing as land, among whom education and culture have become almost synonymous with landlessness.

—*Aldo Leopold, from* A Sand County Almanac

A central focus of my teaching has been to guide my students towards the inexorable connection between the state of their soul and the state of the planet. Significantly it's not so much the scary statistics on ecological devastation that inspire this connection, but rather something much more personal links their soul to the soul of the earth. Often this connection comes in a moment of particular beauty that captures our imagination—the pink radiance of dawn, the luminous shafts of sunlight in a forest, the immense orange of a full harvest moon, a tender moment with a creature, or the immediate healing that comes from swimming in the sea. Sometimes it comes as spiritual practice deepens our connection to the whole.

In this excerpt from Kathie's journal she describes the way many of us separate ourselves from the earth's suffering. Then as her spiritual practice deepens she realizes that she can't separate from something she is part of, and in this moment she finds her personal link to the earth's story.

I have never been an activist about the environment. I have not really understood the passion that some feel about pollution, global warming, and the wholesale destruction of the planet. I knew of the suffering of the earth in a general way, but I have kept my distance. The problem's too big; I don't know what to do; others will take care of it; I'm not a leader; I'm afraid to come face-to-face with it. Besides, our planet's crisis is best left to the scientists and politicians who know what they're doing. This is how I've looked at the problem, and in stating it so, I was off the hook; I was safe. There was no responsibility. I didn't have to learn anything new. I didn't have to take action. I didn't have to feel. I chose ignorance and I set myself apart.

But as I've made progress on my spiritual journey, I realize that the planet's health and my soul's health are inseparable. When I choose ignorance and isolation in relationship to the earth's suffering, I deaden my soul. Without my passion and caring the planet's wounds deepen, and so do mine. Now, I take new steps to connect myself with the earth. I am reading and educating myself about sustainability and finding the pleasure of living more simply. I continue to make my house more environmentally friendly, and tell others about the ecological resources in our community. And I bring the suffering of the earth to my attention through prayer and meditation. As I've rekindled the fire of my caring, it's affected my passion for all of life.

Kathie came to understand the fundamental connection between her suffering and the earth's suffering. As long as she deadened her feelings about the planet's crisis she also deadened her soul. As we so poignantly learned with society, the more we try to isolate ourselves from the suffering of the world the more we suffer. The more we open our hearts to feel the pain the more connected, courageous, and alive we feel. As Kathie awakens her caring for the earth there is a blossoming of passion in other areas of her life. Yet another reminder of the intimate relationship between passion and compassion.

Sometimes our personal connection with the earth comes in a moment of heartbreak. Such a moment came for me on the small island off the coast of North Carolina where David and I take retreat every summer. This is a place of pristine beauty where miles of isolated white powder beach hug the wild maritime forest, a sanctuary for dozens of species of birds. It is also a sanctuary for us—a place to empty out, to find rejuvenation and fresh perspective. Our restoration comes especially from the hours of floating in the warm ocean during the hot summer months.

One day a dead baby whale had washed up on the beach. When the resident naturalist studied the dead whale he found bottles, nylon rope, trash bags, a plastic buoy, and Styrofoam in its stomach. The whale had starved to death because it had no room for food. The whale's starvation caused by human garbage linked my story to the earth's story at a new level. The contrast between the baby whale's death and my rejuvenation in this creature's natural habitat was especially heart wrenching for me.

Occasionally we're blessed to have an experience of oneness with the natural world that is so profound that we literally merge with the story of the earth. It's no longer possible to think or feel that we're separate. Gary had such an experience in Muir Woods. As you read this passage be aware of the similarities with Gary's childhood woods where he became one with stardust.

I had returned to my beloved Muir Woods. I found a trail leading up, away from the crowds, toward the sky. Almost immediately I found a strange feather, perhaps from a hawk, like a sign. As I rounded a switchback on the trail, I suddenly felt as if I had entered a larger dimension. The trail was no longer just ahead of me, but I surrounded it, and could see it as if I was looking from many angles back toward myself.

I suddenly realized that I was the forest! Not just the trees, but the water, the stones, the insects, the animals, the birds, even the sky. I also felt like I didn't need to come back. As if I had "gone home" and become part of everything. I dissolved into the wonder around me. The feeling was so strange that even now I struggle to describe it. I wasn't just out-of-my-body, I was into all that is. I became frightened, elated, sad, and filled with joy all at the same time. Then a pair of hummingbirds arrived and brought me back. On my return hike I found over a dozen feathers scattered all along the way as if to assure my safe way down the trail.

As a young boy and now as a grown man Gary has been blessed to experience how inseparable his story is with the earth's story. As we'll see in later chapters this awareness has lead Gary to both a great reverence and an active responsibility toward the environment.

For many of us the most profound link to the earth comes through an experience of healing. In such an experience we're not only connected to the earth's story, the landscape actually changes and informs our personal story in a fundamental way. The outer landscape offers a way to see inside our soul in a powerful and imaginative way.

Some years ago I experienced this kind of healing from the land in Ireland. I had traveled to Ireland on a pilgrimage to understand my Irish roots and especially to understand my mother in some new way. I arrived in June when everything was in full blossom and the green of the Irish countryside dazzled me.

One day I started out with a small knapsack and journal to spend the afternoon walking through the countryside. As always, I experienced my hiking as prayer, full of awe at the creation and gratitude for the privilege of this life. Walking through the fields of sheep and the jagged beauty of Irish stone walls I came across a wild fruit tree in full bloom; white blossoms like a fragrant cloud floating in the midst of the verdant fields. As I approached the tree there was a round opening in the ground, like a small womb in the earth. I went down into this grassy opening and lay down to rest with blue sky ceiling above me.

No sooner had I closed my eyes than I experienced my mother's presence next to me; clearer than I had felt her in a long time since her death over twenty years before. I felt an overwhelming sadness for all the things we would never share; my husband David, my beloved mountain home and community of friends, my work in the world, and the rich and meaningful life that she had helped inspire. My grief poured forth as I lay on the very land of her heritage. It was a full grief that cleansed me and released me from my mother in a new way. I felt as if finally, now that I had connected with her roots, I could let her go.

The earth reflects and heals us in ineffable ways. The Irish landscape offered me a sacred womb protected by a wild fruit tree where I could finally say good-bye to my mother.

The beginning of stewardship as spiritual practice is the recognition that our destiny is linked with the fate of the earth. How we live today affects the future of all living creatures. This awareness is the doorway to ecological compassion. When our story joins the story of the planet we are inspired to quest for compassion toward the earth that is as vividly experienced as our caring for other people and ourselves. When we are connected to the landscape through beauty, heartbreak, or healing, the circle of compassion is forever expanded to include our nonhuman cousins. Now we have the moral inspiration to practice sustainable living as a path of mindfulness.

Exercise: Finding the Personal Link

Using your chosen spiritual practice, take about fifteen minutes to quiet your mind and open your heart. As you enter your practice, focus on your connection to the whole. Now feel the hard edges of your ego that separate you from the earth begin to soften. Place your hands on your heart and ask your open heart about your connection with the earth. Take time to reflect, draw, and journal.

Let your imagination free-associate moments of particular beauty where you felt connected to the natural world—a sunset, mountain hike, ocean, forest, creature, waterfall—it could be anything. How do you experience your connection? Can you feel your connection with the natural world in the same way you relate to an aspect of beauty within yourself, or another person you care for? Take time to reflect, draw, and journal.

Once again quiet your mind and open your heart. Now recall a moment of personal heartbreak as you connected with the natural world—a poisoned river, raped land, an injured or dead animal, or a battered forest. How did you experience your connection with the earth in that moment of heartbreak? Can you feel how similar this heartbreak is to the pain in your own story and society's story? Can you feel the unbroken whole as you link your story to the beauty and the heartbreak of the earth's story? Take time to reflect, draw, and journal.

Now recall a time when you were healed in some way by the earth. A time when the outer landscape helped you see inside your soul in a way that changed you and informed your story. Perhaps the natural world offered you solace in time of sadness, or clarity in time of confusion. How did you experience your connection with the earth in that moment of healing? How did this affect your desire to return that healing by living in a way that is sustainable and compassionate to the earth.

One way to continue to join your story with the earth's story is to simply focus on one moment of connection each day. You can do this outside in the natural world or as a part of your daily spiritual practice.

SUSTAINABLE LIVING AS A PATHWAY TO MINDFULNESS

How we hold the simplest of our tasks speaks loudly about how we hold life itself. How then do we "come home" spiritually and dwell there? Increasingly it is for me a matter of being willing "to be in place," to enter into deeper communion with the objects and actions of a day and allow them to commune with me.

—*Gunilla Norris, from* Being Home

In her beautiful book, *Being Home*, my dear friend Gunilla Norris offers us the key to experiencing sustainable living as a pathway to mindfulness. It is the degree of mindfulness that we bring to our most ordinary daily acts of sustainability—planting a garden, composting, conserving water and energy, carpooling—that determine the sacredness of living. Indeed it is mindfulness that transforms the mundane into the sacred.

When we experience sustainable living as ongoing practice in mindfulness, suddenly it's not just ecological awareness, but equally spiritual practice. The recycling bins become daily rounds of earth awareness; the water and energy saved are prayers of gratitude; the rides shared become a collective offering to clean fresh air. The act of carefully removing the cellophane window off the cardboard box before putting it in the recycling bin strikes me as no different than mindfully following my breath during meditation, or taking the time to carefully listen to a friend in need. Each of these is a mindfulness practice, each is an act of compassion.

When my students ask me how to integrate sustainable living with spiritual practice I remind them that, like all compassion, ecological compassion begins at home. I guide them to begin in their homes with a mindful evaluation of how they are using the earth's precious resources on a daily basis. I invite them to use David's motto for a responsible citizen "What I bring into my home I steward," and I encourage them to remember that creating a sustainable lifestyle is the single most powerful way we ordinary citizens can make a difference in the future quality of life on this planet. And learning to walk the path of stewardship is for all of us—parents, children, business people, activists, and concerned citizens—who understand that the way we live either contributes further to our ecological crisis, or becomes a central part of its resolution.

My students and I have made a conscious effort to see our daily acts of sustainability as ongoing mindfulness practice. Using the four primal elements—fire, water, air, and earth—we have used the focus: mindfulness transforms the mundane into the sacred. This first excerpt is from Sonya's journal as she continues to explore her relationship with fire, this time from an ecological perspective.

Sunlight streams in through the bedroom window, across my covers and onto my eyelids, waking me with a warm, gentle good morning. I smile, remembering a phrase my mother frequently used when I was a young child, "The sun will come back and you will have another day to play." Somehow this statement gave me great comfort and reassurance.

Further along in my childhood I began to fathom that the sun actually doesn't go away, it's always shining, giving us light. The comfort I felt as a child turned to incredible awe and a sense of wonder that has persisted into my adulthood. Each second the sun transforms four million tons of itself into light, which it scatters in all directions, and some of it lands on my eyelids in the morning. Yet despite the awesome reality that the sun's fire is an ongoing giveaway of energy, I sometimes forget.

In my forgetfulness, I turn on lights when I don't need them and take the gift of light for granted. I mindlessly turn up my thermostat and take the gift of warmth for granted. I glibly heat my food ignoring that the nourishment for my body, my thoughts, and my dreams comes from the relationship between the earth and the sun. In my forgetfulness I become one more haphazard consumer of energy disconnected from the process of life.

Then an evening comes, and as the sun is setting, I hesitantly wonder what would happen if tomorrow the sun didn't rise? How reliant I am on those exploding flames millions of miles away! The last rays of the sun's roaring generosity fills my questioning heart with an unconditional love too great to be contained. In that moment I realize my love is made visible by the simplest of my daily actions: changing light bulbs to be more energy efficient becomes an act of deep gratitude; putting on a sweater rather than pushing up the heat expresses my connection to the earth's well-being; insulating my house is an offering to the great fireball that keeps me alive.

Sonya reminds us how easy it is to take for granted the earth's stupendous generosity. Her humble, sustainable actions become offerings of gratitude and connection. Her mindfulness turns energy-saving actions into prayers of reverence to the great fireball that sustains all of life. She shows us that it is mindfulness that gives us the true perspective of our place in the great web of life. Judith continues to explore the sacred in daily life as she considers the element of water.

I've never thought much of drought. When I was nine, the Maine summer was dry. In the overgrown corner, between the shed and barn, the galvanized washtub stood guard under the gutter spout. After each shower or thunderstorm we'd hoist buckets of tepid water and strain it through a piece of old bed sheet. Bits of blossoms, bugs, blades of grass were captured in the cloth and shaken back to earth behind the shed. The rainwater was silky soft for our shampoos. My brothers and I stood in line, sharing turns from the common tub. Afterwards, we'd haul buckets with spent suds out to the garden. Lettuce and beans perked to attention, glad for our offering. That was long ago.

Nowadays our well could probably support more carelessness, but I am grateful for that drought and the rainwater washtub. Today, in the corner by the kitchen sink, a green spackle bucket sits at attention. It is in the way. This is helpful for remembering. For remembering that water is the substance of life, and that I, like the earth, am two-thirds water; for remembering gratitude for our abundance.

It's hard to say how much water goes down our drain each day—cold water runs as we wait for hot dishwater, or hot water down the drain until its coolness satisfies us that it's perfect for a drink. The green bucket accepts water without judgment. Cool water, water floating with bits of rice and lettuce rinsed from the dinner plates, tepid water, water from the cockatiel's drink dish, the last remaining swigs from the lunch glasses, even water from rinsing the cat's food bowl—all are gratefully held by the green bucket.

Then off I go, bucket in hand, lugging a treat for the thirsty plants. Inside the house, Grandma Ivy's jade tree, the cacti, and other houseplants seem to relish new flavors of brew. Outside the dining room window, blueberry bushes and new juniper shrubs guzzle the wet offering. There is so much more to mindfulness than my formal meditation practice. I need to trip on the green bucket—reminding me how I depend on the earth for my water, reminding me to ponder my own abundance, connecting me with the many others who are suffering from drought or polluted water.

Judith's contemplation on water is a veritable description of stewardship as spiritual practice. She asks us to consider how much we mindlessly waste—whether it's water or anything else. She offers an imaginative and simple response to the waste—a green spackle bucket graciously collecting the unused water and offering it back as nourishment to the plant life. Then she illuminates the very heart of spiritual practice as the awareness of her own abundance connects her to those millions worldwide who are suffering and dying from drought and poisoned water.

Most importantly Judith reminds us that any spiritual practice is deepened in the concentration of formal practice, but is tested and made real in the ordinariness of daily living. It is at this juncture when a mundane act of daily living—conserving water, listening to someone in need, letting go of self-judgment—is experienced through the lens of mindfulness that we enter the territory of the sacred. We shift now from water to the element of air as George continues to ask what can we do, and how can we connect with the earth's suffering.

When a yellow-black cloud of smog blots the air, I feel bad. I think of myself, in the plane or car, as a contributor and ask myself, "What must I do? How must I be? How am I connected?"

159

The Out-Breath: Caring for the World

When the air brings me the smell of lilacs or jasmine or sage, I feel wonderful and I look to find the source. When it's a feedlot, I hold my breath and roll up the windows. When the air moves against me, I am always excited and feel alive. I can remember, as a child, playing a game of leaning into the wind as far as I could and having it hold me up. The stronger the wind, the better.

Carbon dioxide, acid rain, holes in the ozone layer, smog, particulates that block out the stars; I know about them. I know my part in causing them. I try not to feel guilty. I am determined to find my place in the solution by taking small humble steps: walking, riding a bike, or taking public transportation when I can; clustering my errands so there's less drive-time, and car pooling helps too.

I want the air to be clean and fresh and clear. Is this wanting, this longing, of value? To my mind it seems not—only results count. But my heart says "Yes!" I am connected, not only by my actions, but by my longing. Thank you, Air. I care for you.

George shows us that ordinary living also connects us to the earth's suffering. He reflects how easy it is to feel guilty or overwhelmed by the immensity and complexity of this suffering. But he also reminds us of the central antidote to overwhelm or inadequacy—mindful humble steps toward the solution. We each take the steps we can toward more sustainable living; we engage our families; we share resources with our friends and neighbors. Soon our mindful steps have led to a different way of living. Just as with spiritual practice many days of simply practicing brings measurable deepening, so too with stewardship many days of simple actions make a genuine difference. In his lovely final lines George concludes that stewardship is a balance of pragmatic action and the tender longing of the heart.

In my own home one of the most eloquent teachers of the sacred in daily life is my compost bin. I've been composting my garbage for many years but only recently did I realize the full implications of this practice. This entry from my service journal brings us to the earth element.

All year long I lug the small green compost bucket full of leftover scraps, carrot peels, tea leaves, and dead flowers out to the compost bin behind our shed. The old bin has been there for many years, odd shaped and dilapidated. On snowy winter mornings I throw on my boots and gloves and take all the organic material that we don't eat and feed it to the compost bin. I know the birds, deer, and small creatures enjoy our leftovers during the cold winter months. The rest is left to freeze in the old bin until the spring thaw. During the hot summer the compost is full of flies and you can see, and smell, the decomposing taking place. In the late autumn when I throw my pumpkins into the bin I silently wonder how something so large and dense will transform into fine dark soil by the spring.

Mostly I take the compost bin for granted. But one morning something happened that changed this. It was a splendid May morning with lilacs and lily of the valley in full bloom. I carried the compost bucket out to the bin on my regular rounds. After dumping the leftovers and stirring the contents of the bin to help the composting process, I checked the bottom layer of the compost to see if the soil was ready for a friend's garden. As I lifted the small gate at the bottom of the bin rich, dark, moist soil fell into my hands. As I cradled the dark earth in my hands I was overwhelmed with gratitude. It was suddenly so clear that God's presence was staring at me. I realized the old bin contained the mystery of life, and held God inside its dilapidated walls. Life into death, death back to life, over and over the cycle repeated itself silently, faithfully, and miraculously.

As I continued to feel the moist earth against my hands I vowed never again to just dump my leftovers into the old bin, but rather to recognize the spiritual practice I was engaged in. This is communion with the mystery as I throw away what I don't eat letting it rot and transform into rich soil that will nourish a garden so that I can eat again. This is daily spiritual practice where I am reminded that my life's nourishment is inextricably linked to the earth that I live on. This practice is a tangible reminder that life and death are a continuous living circle that I am part of. At that moment, intoxicated by the thick spring air and the dark earth alive in my hands, I knelt next to the old misshapen compost bin and offered prayers of amazement.

Fire, water, air, and earth—without them there is no life. Yet so often we take them for granted. If you're lucky certain moments of startling awareness will wake you out of your trance, and like me, you might find yourself overwhelmed with gratitude for the earth's patient, miraculous, and forgiving generosity. Like Sonya, Judith, and George you might realize that your gratitude comes fully alive as you take the humble, mindful steps to live more lightly on our planet. And over time your ordinary acts of sustainability become sacred offerings to the living earth.

WEAVING THE PATTERN TOGETHER

Over time mindfulness weaves the separate threads of sustainable living into a pattern of ecological beauty and integrity. The weaving is much larger than the individual threads of awareness or the initial effort required to put them together. This is a sure sign that stewardship and spiritual practice are coming together.

After some years of practicing a sustainable lifestyle there are some distinct patterns in my weaving. David and I have created our home with Zen simplicity. We treasure a few beautiful things from our world travels—a rug from Tibet, a hand-carved Balinese statue on our hearth, and a Chinese landscape from a colleague in Shanghai. Recycling bins are tucked away in every corner. Incorporating the splendid large stones on our property we landscaped several small Japanese gardens that require almost no care and very little water. Each garden offers a place of contemplative stillness. When people come to our home they often experience feelings of relief and spaciousness provided by the peaceful simplicity. Beyond the essentials of life we seem to buy fewer and fewer things— books, music, or fresh flowers.

My neighbor Jeanne and I decided to eliminate paper and plastic from our community gatherings. We lend each other plates, glasses, silverware, and cloth napkins. This inspired Jeanne to make a beautiful handmade wicker basket to carry our wares back and forth. I arrange my weekly errands so I need one trip to town instead of three. Fewer car trips means less air pollution, but it also means I have more time for things like reading or being with friends. As I do my errands the shopkeepers recognize me by my grimy cloth shopping bags and Tupperware containers. By my estimation this trusty paraphernalia saves several trees a year, and dozens of pounds of plastic from the landfill.

This weaving of sustainable living is a work in progress. It didn't happen all at once and it's continually evolving as we add new threads of awareness to our lifestyle. It's a daily practice made up of humble acts that simplify our life, offering the gifts of time, community, and creativity. By using less we end up with so much more. Walking the path of stewardship we take it one day at a time just as we do with our spiritual practice. We aspire toward a fresh beginner's mind as we compost, plant trees, shop with green values, conserve, recycle, reuse, and repair. Just like practice we discover both pleasure and challenge. Gently, inexorably, both our practice and our stewardship are changing us and changing the world.

This path of stewardship puts us in harmony with a vast, eternal rhythm of compassion that cares not just for us, not just for now, but for the earth and all its future inhabitants. Living in harmony with this vast rhythm rewards us with an incomparable sense of well-being.

Exercise: Transforming the Mundane into the Sacred

Close your eyes, quiet your mind, and gently follow your breath until you begin to relax.

As you become still, open your heart and focus on this phrase: "my mindfulness transforms the mundane into the sacred." Now keeping your focus—"my mindfulness transforms the mundane into the sacred"—visualize yourself in your house recycling, reusing, repairing, or composting. Imagine each of these as prayers of gratitude for the earth's stupendous generosity. You are offering a gift in return for all you have been given.

Now turn your attention to the sacred element of water. Imagine each shorter shower, every time you don't needlessly flush the toilet or leave the water running, or ignore a leak— each of these connects you with those millions of people who don't have enough water. Each of these savings is offered to those who are dying or suffering from drought or polluted water.

Now bring your attention to the sacred element of fire. Imagine each time you lower the heat, use less air conditioning, get an energy audit for your house, or use energy efficient light bulbs—you offer prayers of reverence to the great fireball that sustains all of life. You recognize your place in the great web of life.

Now you focus on the sacred element of air. Visualize each car pool or ride on public transportation, every walk or bike ride, every time you cluster your errands and drive less—you make an offering to clean, fresh air. You are saying to your family and loved ones, "I want you to breathe free and easy."

Now you focus on the sacred earth element. Imagine that each time you realize you don't need to buy something you help break our collective addiction to consumerism. Every time you choose an earth-friendly product, paying attention to quality and packaging, each time you share, loan, or swap instead of buy—you are offering reverence to the earth. You are saying to those not yet born in the generations who follow you: I care about you, I want you to have abundant resources to enjoy the miracle of life.

If you are not in the habit of thinking about earth sustainability, be gentle with yourself and take small steps. This exercise becomes real only when you practice it over an extended period of time. If you are dedicated to bringing mindfulness to your everyday sustainable acts, you will find that your stewardship becomes a part of your spiritual practice.

Twelve

MY HEART IS BREAKING,
MY HEART IS AWAKENING

Nonviolence does not mean nonaction. Nonviolence means
we act with love and compassion. The moment we stop acting, we undermine the principle of nonviolence.
—*Thich Nhat Hanh, from* Living Buddha, Living Christ

To open to the world's pain, we move gently, allowing our
compassion to blossom in a natural way. We can't force this
process, rather we need to take our time, exploring our own
feelings at a pace that feels natural to us. We continue to cultivate our chosen daily practice as an essential anchor. Over
time we grow stronger and more open. In this mature phase
of service as spiritual practice, we are no longer defended,
and now we are able to move into the deepest waters of compassion.

Along with our capacity to open deeply comes heartbreak. And as great spiritual traditions have taught, there is
purification in this. As our heart shatters so does the hard
shell of our ego. We experience a cleansing—a washing away
of illusions—a letting go of irrelevant aspects of life. This
broken heart refines and liberates us. In this chapter we'll see

how this liberation takes place through human interaction, and in the next chapter we'll witness the heartbreak of ecological compassion.

We'll start with Kathie as she cares for Rose.

When I arrived Rose was in the kitchen trying to cook her breakfast in the microwave. She was all bent over, shaky. She talked of her bad night, of waking early with the nerves in her leg "jumping all over." She had lain awake, cried, and beat the mattress and felt pain, frustration, fear, and loneliness, all in one moment. She told me she sometimes thinks of throwing out her pills, and then she burst into tears. My heart broke as I held her and encouraged her not to discard these feelings as silly or unimportant.

The beauty of this interaction is that Kathie doesn't try to fix Rose, instead she is present. She encourages Rose to open to her pain, to let her heart break as a gateway to real healing. We see Kathie's humanity as she lets Rose into her heart and is willing to feel her losses with her. Once again we witness the mutuality of both suffering and release.

Bridget moved out of her comfort zone when she volunteered as a "big sister" to a seven-year-old named Jerry Anne. This girl's life seemed unimaginable to Bridget. By society's standards Jerry Anne is the product of a "white trash" welfare family, where each of the five children has a different father. Bridget describes her encounter.

Our conversations go like this:

"What's your favorite class in school?"
"I don't know."
"Really? Surely there must be one you like."

"Oh, yeah, gym!"
"So what's your favorite sport?"
"I don't know."
"Do you like art?"
"I don't know."
"What do you like to do?"
"Watch TV."

I think, my God, my work is cut out for me. How do I convince this girl that we could have fun together, laugh, play, read, and go off on adventures. Why do I feel this overwhelming feeling of inadequacy and the need to prove to her that I, Bridget, am not square but in fact quite a hipster. I'm an artist, I drive a cool truck (she said so already), I'm from New York City, know hip-hop music, and am a hot ticket. What more could you ask for from a big sister?

One Saturday afternoon we went to an ice skating show. We watched the performance for two hours. No words were exchanged but she seemed to be enjoying it. We drank hot cocoa and shared a blanket. I finally asked her how she liked the show, and she said it was okay.

Then it was time to take Jerry Anne home. I dropped her off in front of her house. I didn't want to go inside and see her parents sitting on the couch watching TV with toys and a real mess all over the floor. As I drove home, it was snowing, and I was shaking. I pulled off the main road onto a side street, parked my truck, and wept.

At last Bridget understands the enormity and complexity of Jerry Anne's pain. This young girl's suffering is so deeply layered that Bridget doesn't know where to begin—except with her own heartbreak. Now she feels Jerry Anne's desperation. This hurts, but it's also the opening for a far more authentic connection. In this shattered place Bridget is no longer separate from

Jerry Anne. This is a good situation for Bridget to practice *tonglen*, breathing in Jerry Anne's suffering with the wish that she be free of her pain, and breathing out, sending love and healing to her.

Heartbreak is an inevitable part of compassion. It opens us and connects us to those we serve. Staying mindful that we can't explain or fix suffering, we find creative ways to cope. We write poems or sonnets, paint, turn to prayer, silence, long-distance running, or spend time in nature. Both creativity and the solitude of retreat allow us to integrate the lessons of the world's pain.

In the compassionate encounters of Kathie and Bridget we feel their hearts break, but then we also see how their hearts are deepening and strengthening. They meet life face-to-face, shedding illusions. In such moments we are naked, stripped of our ego defenses. In this vulnerable state, cleansing and purification can take place and lead us through another gateway in our spiritual development.

MY HEART IS AWAKENING

As we unearthed the broken heart in our own story we learned that how we related to our brokenness determined whether our heart awakened or closed. We realized that when we offered our personal pain to the great ocean of suffering that we found meaning in the wounds of our story. The significance of this critical lesson comes fully alive as we encounter the world's suffering.

As the heart breaks in the heat of service we find moments of numinous connection where all suffering meets and joins in a great ocean. Here we abandon ourselves to simply being with another's suffering. We recognize we are in the presence not of his or her or its suffering, but "our" suffering. Finally, we realize the utter futility of trying to separate from or defend against something that we are part of. To abandon others in their suffering is to abandon ourselves. To open to the immensity of others' pain is to open to the immense compassion within ourselves. At this juncture our service and our spiritual practice meet as one. And our personal brokenness joins the unbroken whole.

The recognition of the unity of all suffering is not an intellectual experience, but rather an unexpected stroke of grace. It is, in part, the fruit of practicing the qualities of mature compassion. As I teach, I am always moved when we touch this place. One woman allowed herself to feel her teenage daughter's pain during the turmoil of adolescence, and then she remembered her own sister's suicide. Finally, both began to blend into the great sea of universal suffering. A woman who had lost a baby entered the same sea, comforting her friends when their child died. She said she "had a visceral experience of all the babies who have been lost." Yet another woman saw two of her beloved sheep eaten by wild dogs. This loss became one with the recent death of her father.

The gift of the awakened heart is that all suffering in some way belongs to all of us. Here we experience the mysterious intimacy that connects us to everything that lives. In this state, our service becomes an offering, a way of giving back to life itself. Chuck discovered this when he became an advocate for Michael, and he began to chronicle the unexpected gifts of their time together. Chuck is a successful international business executive who has engaged in service as a way to deepen his compassion.

Michael was a successful stockbroker before he became paralyzed from the neck down in a motorcycle accident. He's now able to spell out words, letter by letter, in order to communicate. I have learned more from Michael than I ever imagined. Today I wrote this tribute to him:

> Teacher
> Showing myself to me
> As I watch my impatience
> As I begin to feel my compassion for you
> Your dogged determination
> To make yourself understood
> I can't begin to fathom
> The lessons *you* are learning
> I am a witness
> But you have deeply touched me
> Letter by letter word by word
> Sentence by sentence
> Story by story.

Chuck felt these lessons were so important that he started to bring his son, Alex, with him on his visits. To Chuck's delight, Alex was relaxed and natural, joking and laughing with Michael and instinctively knowing what to say. Children are often refreshingly unself-conscious, in touch with what makes others sad, and able to offer an unfiltered and tender compassion. People who have involved their families in their service, have always found their children bring a special joy to the encounter.

Cece is the mother of two teenagers and an active volunteer. She cares for her mother who has had a severe stroke, works with Holocaust survivors, and holds severely ill babies at the Children's Hospital. Cece explains how her service has awakened her heart and allowed her to experience the unity in all suffering.

As I walk down the corridor, I wonder which babies are most in need of holding today. First, I look for Melissa because I enjoy her so much. I begin with her because she gives me inner strength and courage to help the other babies. Many are unresponsive or very difficult to be with due to the severity of their illnesses.

As I look across the room, I see Kirk. Instinctively, I realize he needs to be held. I know this because a large part of me doesn't want to do this. He is difficult to look at with his facial features hardly recognizable. I go to pick him up. His eyes remain closed or unfocused. No response.

Kirk's nurse enters the room and expresses her gratitude that someone is finally holding him. She says he doesn't get held enough, and offers me a rocker. As I rock, I ask for help and strength to be really present. It is so easy to give up and think that this baby doesn't even know I am here. But I also realize that on some mysterious level, he does know I am here. I follow his breath. I sing his song. I search for skin to touch. So much tubing, so much swelling. I hold him close.

> I am, we are
> I feel, we feel
> I cry, we cry
> We connect.

Cece's fearless heart takes her into the fierce heat of suffering. Holding Kirk, following his breath, she passes through a gateway to the place where all of life connects. There are certain rare moments when suffering transforms us, and we feel the strange beauty of it all. We can accept life just as it is at the same time, we try to alleviate the pain. We learn to live between the opposites of compassionate acceptance and full engagement.

The person who taught me the most about the awakened heart was my cherished friend, Peter, who died of AIDS. The last year of Peter's life was both extremely difficult and meaningful for me. During that time, suffering and beauty lived together under the same roof, and people in my community came forward to help in the most moving ways.

Peter refused to lose hope as he battled his illness. The day before he began his chemotherapy for AIDS-related lymphoma, he invited friends to his house for a ceremony, as he shaved his head in preparation for his treatments. He told us he had always wanted to look like a monk. As the months wore on and he grew weaker, he said to me, "Now I am becoming an advanced monk—no sex, hardly any food, and I pray all the time." I laughed at his wry humor, then I went home and wept.

It was giving to others that helped Peter sustain hope and transcend his constant physical discomfort. He continued working as a psychologist and activist. When I was visiting him in the hospital, just ten days before he died, another man with AIDS was admitted and placed in the bed next to him. Immediately Peter began to comfort the young man's mother. He offered her a copy of his book, *Alive and Well: A Path for Living in a Time of HIV.* Peter was too weak to sign the book, so he asked me to be his proxy. His heart kept opening, and he kept teaching me. At times his teaching was more than my heart could bear, as this journal entry shows.

I take the two-hour trip on the Trailways bus to New York City and on the way in I feel numb. In "death and dying lingo" I am smack in the middle of denial. I have visited Peter often in the hospital, but now he is home with his partner, Tim.

As I enter Peter's room, it's very still, as if he is shuttling back and forth between worlds trying to decide whether to surrender to death or fight for life. His six-foot-four-inch body is even more emaciated. He is unshaven and gaunt. I have known him as a handsome and elegant man.

We hug one another. "Sweet Gail," he says, "it's good to see you." We chat for a little while about a Broadway show we want to see together. Then I go out to do some errands for Tim and Peter. When I return we only have a little time before I have to catch my bus. In two days I am leaving to lead a seminar in Europe. I am fully aware that Peter could die while I am away. As we hug good-bye I tell him how much I love him and whatever happens now it's okay with me. I ask him what prayers he would like. He asks that I pray for strength, clarity, love, and God's presence. I try to hold back my tears but find it impossible.

I leave his apartment, feeling as if I had entered a force field of sorrow that I will never get out of. As I get on the bus, it's as if a cork was pulled, and out pour all my feelings of sadness, rage, despair, confusion, and helplessness. They spill from me reckless and out of control. I feel my deep love for Peter; how rare it is to find a friend who encourages the best in you and isn't afraid to name the worst. I remember all our outrageous adventures, and my heart breaks as I grasp that there won't be any more.

I am sitting on the Trailways bus, tears streaming down my face, when a doorway opens inside me. I go through the door and remember my mother and father's death, as well as the loss of other loved ones. Then I feel all of death stretched out before me. I feel the unspeakable suffering of the holocaust, of centuries of genocide, child abuse, and torture. I feel the earth's unbearable suffering, and I touch the depth of my own pain. Suddenly I know that it's all the same, like a great ocean. And then I experience the strange beauty of it all.

An experience like this doesn't come often, but when it does we are changed forever. Perhaps the only appropriate response is gratitude, along with a genuine attempt to incorporate this knowledge into our lives. Through his startling courage Peter helped me face pain, and he showed me that below the surface of suffering there is something much greater to be learned. Here contradictions disappear—hope and despair, joy and sorrow, unify. We burn away the trivial, the unnecessary, and come closer to the essence of life.

Exercise: My Heart Is Breaking, My Heart Is Awakening

For this exercise put on some music that connects you to your heart and takes you deep into your feelings. Then close your eyes, quiet your mind, and gently follow your breath until you begin to relax. Take a few minutes and go back to your life story to review the exercise where you unearthed your own broken heart. Recall that it was your willingness to feel the pain of your brokenness that allowed healing to take place. In your healing you realized we all are broken. Remember that it was your passion to awaken and find freedom that gave you the courage to pick up your broken pieces and make something new and meaningful. Now you can use this same strength and wisdom to help you face the heartbreak in caring for others and for the earth.

Visualize a specific life situation where there is profound suffering. A person in your family, at work, or a situation in society. Choose something very real for you, something that breaks your heart. Now come face-to-face with the suffering and imagine your heart as a beautiful flower of compassion. Visualize your heart of compassion blossoming naturally, opening gently and at your own pace. No need to force or rush. What do you experience as you gently open your heart to this situation? Take time to reflect, draw, and journal.

Once again follow your breath to quiet your mind. Visualize your heart of compassion blossoming more and more. Now imagine your heart of compassion in full blossom, completely open. No defending, avoiding, or intellectualizing. Once again come face-to-face with the suffering. Open and feel your pain, fear, despair, and helplessness. No fixing or controlling, just let your heart break. Let go and let the pain break your heart. Stay face-to-face with the suffering. Keep following your breath, making room for your heartbreak. Pray for courage if you need it. Take as much time as you need to feel, reflect, draw, and describe your heartbreak in your journal.

Visualize that in the process of your heartbreak with suffering, a cleansing is going on, washing away your illusions. Become aware that as your heart shatters so does the hard shell of your ego. Imagine your broken heart purifying and refining you. What do you experience as you imagine yourself being cleansed, shedding illusions, meeting life face-to-face as you encounter the deepest suffering? Take time to journal.

And now your heart whispers to you that there's an even greater awakening. Imagine a sacred gateway in the center of your heart in full blossom. You go through the sacred gateway and enter a numinous place where all suffering meets and joins, like a great ocean. Visualize the encounter with suffering from this exercise joining with your own suffering, that of your family and friends, community, society, and the world at large. Imagine it all joining like a great ocean. In this unified place can you experience all suffering as "ours"? Can you experience a deeper significance, the possibility that suffering in its true meaning transforms us? What else do you feel in this place where all suffering joins and becomes one? Take time to reflect, draw, and journal. When you have finished this exercise take some time to read it over, reflect on your answers, and allow some time to digest what you have learned.

Thirteen

SEEING THE INVISIBLE THROUGH THE EYES OF THE HEART

Form is certainty. All nature knows this, and we have no
greater adviser . . . in the blue water see the dolphin built to
leap, the sea mouse skittering, see the ropy kelp with its air-
filled bladders tugging it upward, see the albatross floating
day after day on its three-jointed wings. Each form sets a
tone, enables a destiny, strikes a note in the universe unlike
any other. How can we ever stop looking? How can we ever
turn away?

—Mary Oliver, from Blue Pastures

In the last chapter we explored the liberation that comes
when we enter the deepest waters of society's suffering,
allowing the heart to shatter and awaken to fuller compassion. This awakened heart was born from passionate engagement with the human family, and now we're asked to fully
encounter the suffering of the earth family.

One of the greatest differences between human suffering
and ecological suffering is that for the most part the earth's
suffering is invisible to us. When we care for a sick child or
sit with a dying person we have a visceral connection with

their pain and often we experience an emotional fulfillment from our caring. Sitting in a natural landscape it's harder to realize how much our earth is suffering from poisoned air and water or abused by overdevelopment.

But when our heart is open we can no longer deny or run away from pain, be it personal, societal, or ecological. The awakened heart feels, connects, shatters; through this engagement the earth's suffering becomes visible, real, and starkly urgent. Indeed we can see the invisible through the eyes of the heart.

And now Mary Oliver's potent question rings at the core of our being "Each form sets a tone, enables a destiny, strikes a note in the universe unlike any other. How can we ever stop looking? How can we ever turn away?"

An essential pathway to compassion for the human family and ourselves is to directly encounter the pain and go through the feelings this aroused. We too must face the suffering in the natural world with a warrior's heart. This is no easier to do with strangled rivers, raped rain forests, or battered wetlands than it is with the human equivalent.

A vivid experience taught me how unified personal, societal, and ecological sufferings are when we engage the world with an open heart. Where I live in the Hudson River Valley I have many special places—mountains, rivers, and trees—that I visit for renewal and spiritual nourishment. One of these special places is a trinity of ancient apple trees bending over a small mountain stream. I've gone there off and on for well over fifteen years. As I rest against them, these wise old apple tree crones have offered me counsel in a myriad of ways and comforted me over the death of a loved one.

My ritual is to approach these apple trees by foot, hiking up the dirt road along the stream. Before visiting with them I always stopped across the road to admire their cousins—a glorious grove of beech, oak, and poplar indigenous to our region. I loved this handsome grove, so strong and sturdy; I always felt restored in their presence.

One day as I hiked up over hill, to my utter amazement the entire grove of trees had been bulldozed. I stood shocked in front of them, sprawled like bloody, dead soldiers on a battlefield. I felt sick and nauseous. I ran across the road and vomited near the old apple trees. Still dizzy, I lay down among the apple trees. Immediately I had a vivid memory of both my gut-wrenching vomiting at the moment of my mother's death, and stopping my car to throw up the day I heard about the Tiananmen Square massacre in Beijing.

Surrounded by the ancient apple trees, I recognized the unity in these three events: my mother's valiant struggle with a mysterious heart disease; the students in Beijing demonstrating for democracy; and the handsome grove of trees so generously offering their healing presence. With each I felt sickened by grief and acutely aware of the inevitable suffering and impermanence of all of life. In some inexorable way my mother, the Chinese students, and the trees were now one for me.

Part of my earth stewardship included staying open and feeling grief stricken at the destruction of the grove of trees I so loved. My awakened heart was familiar with that place where all suffering joins and becomes one, and now the trees joined with my mother and the Chinese students. The trees too were citizens of a great community of life—humans, animals, mountains, rivers, stars, and sky. Indeed, we are all wild and mysterious creatures with invisible threads connecting us in our joy and our suffering.

Just as I have encouraged my students to face both personal and societal suffering, I have also asked them to encounter the heartbreak of the earth. Part of the spiritual practice of stewardship is to open to the myriad of primal feelings like rage, despair, grief, and helplessness in the face of our damaged earth. The more we're aware of the kind of trouble the planet is in, the more we have to face these emotions. If we shut down our feelings then once again we're cut off and separated. To break the cycle of separation—be it alienation from self, society, or the earth—we need to stay open and feel the suffering. Rumi gives us courage when he says, "Pilgrimage to the place of the wise is to find escape from the flame of separation."

Using the focus, my awakened heart makes visible the suffering of the earth. I asked my students to choose some part of the natural world and connect with the pain. In this journal entry, Gary connects with outrage and despair in a northern forest.

> The northern forest speaks to me.
> My life as forest
> Habitat life
> Turning raindrops to sap
> Sunlight into leaves
> Mountains to soil
> Everything is alive!
> My anger is sadness
> I am almost speechless.
> You fill my hair with strings
> And leave cans in my belly,
> Your waste I cannot turn into life.
> If I slaughtered your children
> As quickly as you kill mine,
> You would cease to exist on the face of this earth.
> Learn respect for me and you will learn respect for
>   yourself.

The Out-Breath: Caring for the World

> Pick the trash out of my heart and you pick it out of
> your soul.

In previous journal entries we have seen Gary's deep affinity with the forest. It's not surprising then that a forest is the place where he experiences the suffering of the earth. We witness Gary's despair as he ponders the damage caused by human garbage and the mass destruction of the planet's forests. As with society, this suffering is too complex to fix, but Gary can stay open and present. He doesn't close down or try to avoid the pain, he lets his heart break. This is a time when he might return to the practice of *tonglen:* breathing in the suffering of the earth with the wish that it be free of pain, and breathing out, sending love and healing.

PROTECTING THE CREATURES

Asking what good are eagles and owls, or ebony spleenworts, or black-footed ferrets, or snail darters, or any other of our fellow travelers, is like asking what good are our brothers and sisters, or children, or friends. Such questions arise only in the absence of love.

—*Scott Russell Sanders*

In walking the path of stewardship we understand how important it is to conserve and protect the land, water, energy, and air. A further aspect of ecological compassion is protecting the earth's creatures. Continuing with the focus, my awakened heart makes visible the earth's suffering, we come to Ann's story as she teaches us about the animals' pain.

Ann has long felt especially attuned to animals. When her beloved cat, Dutchess, died in her arms, Ann's stewardship of the creatures became an integral part of her spiritual practice. During her time of loss Ann felt a sense of mission, a desire to give back to the creatures as a way to honor Dutchess. She has since become a leading advocate for the animals in her community. Ann's stewardship has led to a passion to educate others about how to protect the animals in their lives.

Ann's passion is to make visible the creatures' suffering, but first she has to feel their pain herself. In this excerpt from her service journal, she quickly learns how ever present suffering is at the animal shelter. And she learns to keep her heart open.

My heart breaks at the suffering so many animals endure, often at the hands of humans. Sheltering homeless, abandoned, and abused animals has become my compassion in action. My compassion has grown as I've learned to encounter the pain in this work: having to euthanize animals that are old, sick, and homeless because there's really no other alternative; the stray ward at the shelter filled to capacity with confused, scared, and lonely creatures; caring for small innocent animals that have been cruelly abused or tortured and whose spirits are so broken I dare not imagine what they've lived through.

But the joyful moments at the shelter are just as vivid: holding, cuddling, and walking the animals and feeling their response to my caring; the days when we can hardly keep up with loving adoptions; a little girl telling her mother she loves her new kitten more than anything in the world; an older man asking for an animal that doesn't have much chance of adoption; a young boy asking me if I'd like to go home with him and see the big country yard for his new dog. I feel the joy and the pain equally, and my tears flow freely. My deepest wish is to provide an experience of love for each animal that I contact—whether its life is long or short.

My other deepest wish is to educate as many people as possible
about how we contribute to animals' suffering in a myriad of ways
that we may not even be aware of. We may love animals and never
intentionally hurt them, yet be unaware that we're using personal or
home care products that are tested through torturing animals. We
can each help alleviate the suffering of all creatures through several
compassionate actions: by loving and respecting the animals in our
immediate environment; by purchasing and using cruelty-free products; and by protecting creatures as members of the family of life
that share this earth with us.

It is the eyes of Ann's heart that allow her to see all the levels
of the animals' suffering—visible and invisible. Ann reminds
us of the intimate relationship between heartbreak, passion,
and compassion in action. She recognizes that the spiritual
practice of stewardship is an equal partnership of joy and sorrow. An awakened heart takes us on an emotional roller
coaster ride where we might witness unspeakable suffering
right next to the precious rewards of service. Susan was also
willing to enter the fire of heartbreak as she focused her service on protecting the winged ones—owls, hawks, and
eagles.

I am a volunteer at a raptor rehabilitation center. I can't claim to
understand the suffering these majestic birds experience. Most of the
birds I work with have been harmed by human activity. Many are in
great physical pain, some heal and return to their habitat, and others
die. Still others are long-term captives, healed on some level but not
released because of their inability to hunt for themselves. Does it
serve creatures of the wild to support their healing and then keep
them in a cages—even if spacious—for the remainder of their lives?
Yet an unanswered question for me.

A few days ago the game warden brought in a great horned owl. One foot is seriously cut, and the bird has been starving. The owl has been to the vet and her foot is wrapped. I'm asked to help with the bird's evening foot soak. Wearing protective leather gloves I unwrap her foot and rest the giant owl's back against my chest. Holding her terribly wounded foot in the warm basin I feel her suffering as if it were my own. I send healing energy and talk to her in a soothing way. Another volunteer and I medicate and wrap the owl's foot. She gulps food from a syringe while I hold her under my arm. I pray that she will heal and be able to return to the wild.

Working with wounded owls and hawks has helped me understand that our suffering is a mirror of the earth's suffering. In healing one we heal the other. I want to open my heart and learn what's behind suffering. Sometimes I find something dark to be faced with presence, courage, and commitment. Other times I find light directly behind the suffering and I want to be open to this light.

In Susan's moving encounter with the giant owl we revisit the core qualities of compassion—an open heart, presence, and humble simplicity. As with human suffering, Susan finds moments of numinous connection when her suffering joins with the bird's pain and she feels the unity of life. As with any profound encounter with suffering, Susan also finds unanswerable questions about the nature of compassion as she cares for the owl. These majestic wounded birds teach us, once again, that there are no simple formulas for compassion. They remind us that when stewardship is held in the context of spiritual practice we learn to let go of our need to control and fix suffering, or to understand it with our rational mind.

Sometimes when we care for a creature or a person, knowing the most loving response is not so straightforward. When a dear friend of mine was dying I constantly struggled about when to encourage her will to live and when to support her in surrendering to the dying process. As a hospice volunteer I've witnessed many families struggle with the same issue. And I've watched friends confront this dilemma as they decide when to euthanize a beloved animal because their suffering is so overwhelming. No one has a simple answer to these questions. In these moments we can return to our chosen spiritual practice, open wide the door of our hearts, and then respond to what's needed with simple presence and loving kindness.

Exercise: My Awakened Heart Makes Visible the Earth's Suffering

An essential pathway to compassion for both yourself and the human family was to directly encounter the pain and go through the feelings this aroused. You too must face the suffering in the natural world with a warrior's heart. Now you can use all you have learned about compassion as you allow the openness of your awakened heart to make visible the suffering of the earth. If it's helpful, you can go back and review the exercises you have already done on unearthing your broken heart and "my heart is breaking, my heart is awakening."

Go to your chosen practice for about fifteen minutes to quiet your mind and open your heart. Then visualize a specific situation where the earth or the creatures are being harmed in some way: poisoned rivers, raped rain forests, strangled air, battered wetlands, abandoned or abused creatures. Choose something very real for you, something that breaks your heart.

Return to the image of your awakened heart, your heart of compassion completely open. No defending, avoiding, or intellectualizing about suffering. Now using the focus—my

awakened heart makes visible the suffering of the earth—
come face-to-face with the situation you have chosen. Open
and feel your pain, grief, rage, or helplessness. No fixing or
controlling, just let your heart break. Let go and let the eyes
of your heart make visible the pain of this situation. Stay
face-to-face with the suffering. Keep following your breath,
making room for your heartbreak. Take as much time as you
need to feel, reflect, draw, and describe the pain of this
encounter.

Keeping your chosen situation in your heart, take a few
minutes to practice *tonglen:* breathing in the suffering of your
encounter with the wish that it be free of pain, and breathing
out, sending love and healing. Breathing in the suffering of
your encounter with the wish that it be free of pain, and
breathing out, sending love and healing. Allow the gentle
practice of *tonglen* to remind you that compassion has no need
to control or fix the suffering of the earth, simply to open to
it and be present with loving kindness.

PART III

Circling Home: When Inner and Outer Unite as One

When the inward and the outward are illumined, and all is clear, you are one with the light of sun and moon. When developed to its ultimate state, this is a round luminosity that nothing can deceive, the subtle body of a unified spirit, pervading the whole universe.

—*Liu I-Ming, from* Awakening to the Tao

INTRODUCTION

Our inquiry into the world's suffering has taken us from the land of moral obligation fraught with egos and shadows, to the territory of effortless generosity. We have seen that with the cultivation of a quiet mind, an open heart, presence, and radical simplicity—serving flows naturally and freely from us. With time these qualities of mature compassion lead to a place where our service and our stewardship become an extension of our spiritual practice. This practice is to open to suffering, to feel it, to connect with it, and to let it flow through. Dedicating ourselves to this practice makes us strong, and when we're strong our heart can break in a particular way that liberates us. As we conclude, our compassion has come into full bloom. Now we see the true nature of suffering and we can respond skillfully to it.

Over time, as we become more competent in caring for our families, colleagues, communities, and environment we notice that we are changing. We begin to know ourselves in fresh and surprising ways. Our relationship with our own suffering evolves, coming into proper perspective as we see how it fits within the larger pattern of the web of life. We realize that the qualities of mature compassion used in caring for all living things are the very things we need for our own soul care. Just as a fierce dedication to a chosen spiritual practice is required for conscious caring, it's also required for our own spiritual health. As we opened the circle of compassion to welcome the land, water, forests, and creatures—we were enriched by this kinship with the many-voiced landscape. And thus the obvious fully reveals itself—the gifts we receive from caring for the world are precious contributions to our own development.

Heather's story illuminates this intimate partnership between inner and outer. Heather is an innovative psychologist whose work emphasizes the healing of the earth and as integral to self-healing. In this passage from her service journal we see how her inner well being is indistinguishable from her outer stewardship of the wooded land near her home. We witness how the woods heal her, and in turn how her fierce dedication to conserve the wooded land is also part of her soul care.

The birch trees shiver in the wind. The beech trees stand stoic and silent in their dark skin, while the pine trees proudly flaunt their lasting green. I stand beside them as we watch the ice begin to form on the edge of the dark pond in front of us. The blue herons have gone now. I hear an osprey call to her mate as they soar from tree to tree around the pond hunting for fish. This same pair was here last fall, and soon, they too will wend their way southward. Many geese have stopped here briefly on their journey to warmer land. Their honking fills the air as they encourage each other on their way.

Together we watch the waves move across the pond and let our roots sink deeply into the moist, rich earth. I let myself remember. My

spirit reaches out and loses its boundaries. I feel the sense of wholeness, of love. For a moment, I lose myself and become part of the
matrix, the great web of life. For a moment, I feel home.

Then off in the distance, I hear the sounds of bulldozers clearing
the land for a new house being built on the edge of these woods. The
web is torn and I feel the chill wind against my skin. Danger
encroaches upon these woods. The deer can feel it. The geese know it.
The trees whisper it among themselves. I pray for guidance on how
to protect this land.

I have attended all the town meetings. I have helped put out a
newsletter about the project to conserve the woods and keep in close
touch with those negotiating to protect this precious land. I have
educated others to send letters and pledge money to the environmental coalition trying to purchase the land. I wait. The land waits.
And I feel full of fear. The land holds me and tells me not to be afraid.
But I don't know how to not be afraid, because I don't know if I can
live if she is destroyed.

I walk to the edge of the pond on the western shore where I have
come for many years to meditate and pray and watch the shifting
moods of the sky and water. I lift my arms to the four directions, to
Father Sky and Mother Earth. The trees breathe out, and I breathe in.
For a moment again, for a precious moment, we are one.

These woods offer Heather spiritual sustenance, she goes to
them in times of joy and sorrow. She and the land belong to
one another. So deep is her attachment that she wonders how
she will go on if she loses the woods she loves. Her fight to
protect the place she belongs to is a fight to protect her own
sense of belonging. For Heather, the inner and the outer have
united as one.

Pat's story is also a stunning portrayal of this seamless
exchange between the in-breath of soul care and the out-breath

of dedicated service. When she retired from a highly successful military career as a colonel, Pat appeared to have it all. But spiritually she was a hostage to a past full of rage and violence. She knew it was time to confront her personal demons. For her service she chose the "Alternatives to Violence Program" in the Maine State Prisons, where in the last six years she has become the leader in expanding the program to women's prisons.

The prisoners have been great teachers; they've shown me that life is an inside job that requires tremendous self-compassion. Through my prison work I am learning to embrace my monsters and let go of a lifetime of suffering. I have seen the beloved in each prisoner in his story of abuse, passion gone awry, or gentle transformation. I have found and laid claim to my own spiritual essence as a result of my prison service.

In listening to these men's stories, I find the same abuse and shame that characterized my early years. My prison teachers are helping me to learn to forgive my father. They are teaching me the price we pay for separation, and the healing that comes through love. In prison, I find the compassion for our human condition. Over and over again I find the very core of my own humanness.

My love of this service—my jail time—is complete. Quite simply, I have found myself through this service. As these men reveal their souls and discover their own personal responsibility for their incarceration, I have found my own commitment to a nonviolent life.

Pat's work in prison healed her and opened the door to her soul. In Part Two, we saw how our personal story comes fully alive only when we connect with the larger story of the world, when we offer the lessons from our saga in service to others. Within this connection, where a personal story meets the eternal story, we could find healing and spiritual wholeness. Pat and Heather's stories are compelling examples of this wholeness that illuminates the full cycle of the rhythm of compassion; in breathing out—reaching towards others, we return to the in-breath of our own soul care.

Like Pat and Heather, many unsung individuals have walked this path of tending to both the inner and the outer life. In these times we need many more with this awareness and commitment. Each time you reach out to make the world a better place you counteract the numbing despair of the morning papers and the evening news. Conversely, each time you are seduced by that despair you become part of the epidemic of cynicism so prevalent today. A cynicism that dehumanizes us, paralyzes us, and deprives of our full range of possibilities.

To engage socially is an act of faith, an exercise of the imagination. During the First Earth Run we honored many people who are working to make the world a better place: people who have chosen vision and ingenuity over cynicism and despair. In small villages in Africa and India and in cosmopolitan cities like Tokyo and London we recognized hundreds of daily acts of compassion that the media usually doesn't cover.

In West Africa, a collective of women built a dam that irrigated enough land to feed several villages during a time of extreme drought. The women had no machinery and built the dam by carrying huge stones on their backs. In Philadelphia, a woman decided to help her troubled son who was hooked on drugs. She cleared out her house and made it a recreation center—a safe haven for her son and his friends. She listened to the kids and treated them with respect and love. She educated them about their choices and gave them hope in their future. They started to care more about life and less about drugs. The word got out and soon she was running a center for inner-city youth. In a small Brazilian village in the Amazon, the community bands together to save the rain forest. They become a model for eco-tourism teaching the importance of protecting diverse species as well as their indigenous way of life. In Malaysia, a group of concerned university students set up a remedial reading program for children who had difficulty learning to read. The program was so successful the First Lady of Malaysia was inspired to find funding and make it a national effort.

These contributions were natural and spontaneous— human nature at its most generous and creative. It is my belief that such actions are utterly contagious; the more we hear these stories, the more we connect with our own desire to give. In *Anything You Love Can Be Changed,* Alice Walker says, "During my years of being close to people engaged in changing the world I have seen fear turn into courage. Sorrow into joy. Funerals into celebration. Because whatever the consequences, people, standing side by side, have expressed who they really are, and that ultimately they believe in the love of the world and each other enough *to be that*—which is the foundation of activism." Let us love the world enough to change it—and be grateful for the ways it changes us.

Exercise: Reaching Out, Returning Inward to the Soul

Close your eyes, quiet your mind, and gently follow your breath until you begin to relax. Your inquiry into the suffering of society and earth has taken you from the land of moral obligation fraught with egos and shadows, to the territory of effortless generosity. You have seen that with the cultivation of a quiet mind, an open heart, presence, and radical simplic-ity—serving flows naturally and freely from you.

With time these qualities of mature compassion lead to a place where your service and your stewardship become an extension of your spiritual practice. Integrating your service with your spiritual practice made you strong enough for your heart to break in a certain way that liberated you. Through all of this you have become more compassionate and more skillful in caring for others, and you have changed. As you have reached out to the world, your soul has been nourished.

Once again follow your in-breath and your out-breath, your in-breath and your out-breath. Now as you respond to these questions begin to follow the full cycle of your rhythm of compassion. Become aware that as you have breathed out—reaching toward others, you have returned to the in-breath of your own soul care. How did you deepen your own self-understanding as you faced your social shadow and the underbelly of your motivation to serve? How are the qualities of mature compassion—a quiet mind, an open heart, pres-ence, and radical simplicity—as important to your own self-compassion as they are in caring for others? Take time to reflect, draw, and journal.

Continuing to follow the full cycle of your rhythm of compassion, ask how your capacity to face suffering without defending, avoiding, fixing, or rationalizing has affected your relationship to your own suffering. From your perspective what are the most precious gifts you have received as you reached out to care for others? Take time to reflect, draw, and journal.

Fourteen

LETTING GO, LETTING GOD: THE DIVINE PARTNERSHIP

God demands nothing less than complete self-surrender as the price for the only real freedom that is worth having. And when a person thus loses himself, he immediately finds himself in the service of all that lives. It becomes his delight and recreation. He is a new person never weary of spending himself in the service of God's creation.

—Mahatma Gandhi

As the inner and outer become more and more unified we feel a profound intimacy with everything that lives, and now our service is an offering to life itself. Our ego has been shattered and burned away. We have made room for a force of far greater magnitude. More and more we find that we are disappearing, and a divine presence is taking over. We understand William Blake's words "I myself do nothing. The Holy Spirit accomplishes all through me." We are growing in our capacity to surrender to God.

Living this beautiful paradox—getting out of the way and doing less, so that a greater presence can flow through us and accomplish more—is an elegant way to care for both soul and

197

society. Our capacity to work in partnership with the divine becomes a direct reflection of a balanced partnership between our inner life and outer engagement with the world. As inner and outer continue to unify we find it is second nature to work in harmony with this presence.

This higher power is called many things by many people. Bede Griffiths wrote in *Returning to the Center* "The ultimate meaning and purpose of life cannot be expressed, cannot properly be thought. It is present everywhere, in everything, yet it always escapes our grasp. . . . We speak of 'God,' but this also is only a name for this inexpressible mystery." I have always told my students I care little what they name this infinite mystery, but I care enormously that they cultivate a relationship with it.

Some people I work with have a devout relationship with their God. Others prefer not to name this presence but they nourish a deep faith through their relationship with the natural world, love of their family, or their work for social justice. No matter what we call it, or don't call it, at a certain point in the human journey this divine partnership becomes a crucial element in caring for the world and ourselves.

Many of us need to do some healing work with a counselor or support group in order to find a mature relationship with our God. Often we have to undo our childhood programming—a belief that God is either punishing and authoritarian, or pampering and indulgent. As we cultivate a more responsible relationship with our God, we no longer view suffering as God's fault, but rather an inextricable part of the human condition. I have found this inner work is critical if we are to grow in compassion and serve more skillfully.

In the following journal entries we see the various ways this divine partnership can manifest. We begin with Melinda, who has suffered from chronic illness much of her life.

As I serve those with chronic illnesses, I am learning to anchor myself first. I reach out to God, and then I reach out a helping hand. Instead of giving to receive, first I receive from God. Then my giving flows more naturally without conditions such as getting love or recognition. For me it's important to call in God for assistance. Then I know I'm not alone and I don't feel responsible to heal others alone.

This divine partnership helps Melinda let go of her ego and of any feeling that she should fix someone or be responsible for another's healing. She's joined with a higher source, and she allows this source to act through her. As a conduit, Melinda feels a loving detachment: a kind of sacred objectivity that permits her to be both more accepting and more honest with those she cares for.

Mary is in her midseventies and beloved by all in her community. She has been involved in a myriad of volunteer activities including hospice, teaching yoga, and elders. Now Mary is helping to ease a friend toward death. She recognizes that to do this, she needs not just a helping hand from social agencies and neighbors, but the support of a higher power.

He has Hodgkin's disease and is drinking a quart of whiskey a day. Not much for me to do but visit, see that his will is in order, and check that the home care worker is coming. He is apt to fire people.

As it was when my father died, it is hard to watch an active, intelligent, ambitious person fade away. The disappearance of wondrous qualities, the overriding emphasis of the daily details of human living, and the inability to communicate on a meaningful level have been overwhelming. I learn ever more clearly that I must repeatedly turn to my God, not in anger, but for a vision of green pastures.

Mary demonstrates the wisdom of an elder. She's fully present to suffering, and when it threatens to overwhelm her, she turns to her God for comfort and for strength. This is crucial to both our spiritual quest as well as our quest to sustain skillful, compassionate service. We must turn to a higher power not in anger at the unfairness of life, but rather for a vision of peace and resolution. This is much like the forgiveness work with our parents where we accepted their imperfections and focused on what we had learned and how we could give back to life. There is a time when we need to heal our relationship with the divine father and mother as well: to accept the conditions of human existence and concentrate on the unfathomable love that is available to us. This kind of relationship with God is never naive or complacent in the face of life's complex challenges, rather it is fully responsible and engaged. Cece demonstrates this maturity.

One day she received a phone call from the Shoah Visual History Foundation, founded and chaired by Steven Spielberg. This foundation was seeking Holocaust survivors interested in recording their eyewitness testimony on videotape. They contacted Cece because her parents were survivors of the camps in Poland. They offered to train her in the interviewing techniques.

My reaction to the phone call was confusing. I felt overwhelmed by excitement and also by a fear of my own inadequacy. There were as many reasons to say yes as to say no. I strongly desired to make some kind of peace with a very difficult part of history. Yet I was afraid of reopening many deep and personal wounds.

I arrived in New York with two hundred other people from all over the country. The training session was superbly organized. We learned how to help the survivor remember as much as possible. We learned what kind of support is helpful and what comments can be detrimental. We viewed many videotapes. (Eleven thousand interviews had already been completed.) We watched a variety of heart-wrenching stories and my heart shattered many times.

It takes courage to face the experience the survivor wants to share, to ask questions, and push into darkness. I wondered, how could I truly listen to a survivor's story without my own sad thoughts coming in? When a survivor breaks down in the devastation of her memories, how can I just be with that? I asked these questions in my prayers. Then finally the answer became clear. I cannot do this alone. It must be in partnership with that holy knowing energy deep within me and all around me. It's time to let go, and let God.

Sooner or later we learn that we can't do it alone. Then we turn to some higher source, whatever we might name it, for support. This is a turning point in our personal journey as well as our capacity to care for others. With this divine partnership we can respond to more of the world's challenges. We continue to fortify this relationship through our chosen spiritual practice. Then as we grow stronger we find that more is asked of us.

I schedule phone sessions with my students in order to support them and stay close to their journeys. One day I witnessed such concentrated suffering that something in me broke. It began with the first phone call. A woman found her husband was unfaithful once again, and she began the process of ending a thirty-five-year marriage. A man's mother died and he needed comforting. Another student finally admitted his addiction to drugs. The next person had just uncovered memories of child abuse, then another told me her son was missing again. Finally there was the discovery of possible breast cancer. Each person was confronting a wild mix of despair, rage, loss, and helplessness.

At the end of the phone sessions, I felt like a whirling dervish, and by now I was spinning out of control. It was clear I couldn't contain this by myself. I was exhausted and in my heart was a terrible heaviness uncharacteristic of me. I went immediately to the meditation room in my house and began to pray. The concentration of my students' pain intensified my prayer and suddenly I found myself on my knees. Fervently I prayed to understand suffering more fully, and to learn to give all suffering to God.

Within a few minutes something unexpected took place. In my mind's eye I saw my students standing in front of me, and I felt my love for them. As the story of their lives unfolded before me, their joys and sorrows appeared as a seamless, unified whole. I saw each of them growing strong and luminous as they fully lived their suffering. Their challenges became a gateway to their liberation and their full becoming. I remembered Simone Weil's words, "Love of God is pure when joy and suffering inspire an equal degree of gratitude."

Exercise: Divine Partnership

Return to your chosen spiritual practice and take about fifteen minutes to quiet your mind and open your heart. Now go back through the sacred gateway of your heart into that place where all suffering meets and joins, like a great ocean. Become aware that in this place of unity the rigid boundaries of your ego that separate people and divide the world no longer exist. Imagine yourself resting in this field of unity. As you rest in this field of unity become aware of how you are disappearing, and a presence—a force of far greater magnitude—is taking over.

How do you experience this presence? Remember you can name this presence whatever is appropriate and authentic for you. Take time to reflect, draw, and journal.

Now visualize yourself caring for someone in your life who is in pain. This could be a person, an animal, or even a poisoned river. As you care for them imagine yourself in direct partnership with this presence of mystery and infinite love. Imagine you are joined as one with this presence. Come face-to-face with this pain and visualize this presence working through you, guiding you, giving you courage, calmness, and profound compassion. How do you experience this partnership? How is it different from when you care for someone or something by yourself, without the support of this presence? How does your partnership with this presence affect the way you serve? Take time to reflect, draw, and journal.

Whenever you find yourself caring for someone or something you can practice deepening your partnership with this presence, allowing it to move through you. And each time you return to your chosen spiritual practice, you fortify this partnership.

Fifteen

THE HEART IN FULL BLOSSOM: MOVING BEYOND RIGHT AND WRONG

There are many ways to search but the object of the search is always the same. Don't you see that the roads to Mecca are all different? . . .The roads are different, the goal one. . . . When people come there, all quarrels or differences or disputes that happened along the road are resolved. . . . Those who shouted at each other along the road 'you are wrong ' or 'you are an infidel' forget their differences when they come there because there, all hearts are in unison.

—*Rumi*

What happens at this phase of our inquiry when inner and outer are in harmony, and increasingly we are working in partnership with a divine presence? Now our heart is in full blossom and more is asked of us. We are asked to face the situations where it is most difficult to find compassion, the places where we are stuck in simplistic right and wrong positions at home, at work, and in our communities. We are asked to face all the messy contradictions and inconsistencies within ourselves and the world. We will need everything we have learned about compassion in order to hold these contradictions and move beyond the tidy universe of right and wrong.

Perhaps the most important mandate in our world today is to practice this full-blooded, robust compassion. His Holiness the Dalai Lama is a consummate teacher of this far reaching spiritual strength. At a conference I once asked him about his remarkable lack of vindictiveness at the Chinese. He responded that "righteousness is an unskillful use of energy, and that compassion is always a good use of energy." In his book, *The Art of Happiness,* he says, "Genuine compassion is based on the rationale that all human beings have an innate desire to be happy and overcome suffering, just like myself. . . . With this as a foundation, you can feel compassion whether you view the other person as a friend or an enemy. It is based on the other's fundamental rights rather than your own mental projection." Through the potent example of his life the Dalai Lama teaches that genuine compassion is utterly inclusive, demanding the most rigorous form of spiritual development

We have seen this kind of genuine compassion as Mili forgave her father for the unspeakable suffering he had caused her. This required time and patience, support from a therapist, ongoing spiritual practice and connection with God, and abundant courage on Mili's part. When I visited China with my citizen diplomacy delegation just after the Tiananmen Square crisis, it was the sustained focus on quieting our minds and opening our hearts that allowed us to hold the widely contradictory opinions rather than demanding simple right and wrong answers.

The still, spacious mind and the awakened heart understand there are no simplistic truths. These sisters of stillness and heartfulness offer caring from a nonjudgmental, unitive place where we're all connected in both our joy and sorrow. When we care for someone with AIDS or cancer, serve in a prison, counsel a person with an abusive childhood, work to protect an endangered species or disappearing wetland, or minister to a battered woman, our compassion is not based on necessarily agreeing with someone else's values. Maybe we hold the same values, maybe we don't. Genuine compassion transcends specific values, and moves into a universal sphere where we are all connected in our desire to be happy and free of suffering.

The spiritual largesse of authentic caring deepens through the practice of facing all the shadow stuff that is the opposite of compassion. It is, just like the rest of our humanity, a beautiful mess. Every time I pick up a beer can carelessly thrown out of a car window I feel furious. When I see snowmobiles damaging forest preserves I get righteous. When I travel through beautiful land that's been overdeveloped my heart breaks. Sometimes my rage is constructive when I use it to fuel my own commitment to teaching others about sustainable living.

But if my righteousness is directed toward making others wrong and me right it's toxic and it wastes my life energy. This is when I need to practice genuine compassion— expanding my heart, returning to that place of spacious stillness where contradictions can coexist. This is not a tidy or rational place—not a place where my intellect is very comfortable. This is the territory I cultivate in my daily meditation practice and prayer life. Thomas Merton helped us when he said in *New Seeds of Contemplation*, "It is in deep solitude and silence that I find the gentleness with which I can truly love my brother and my sister." It's also here, in the solitude of spiritual practice, that I can accept myself both when

I'm furious as well as when I'm equanimous with those who have different values than I do.

As part of their process of deepening I have asked my students to consciously face the situations where they find it most difficult to feel compassionate. I have reminded them that it is especially in these difficult experiences where we hold different values that the heart stretches larger to hold more caring. In this passage as Susan faces her righteousness, she turns to prayer to help her expand beyond right and wrong. Her journal entry is written as a free-form loving-kindness prayer to the contradictory forces she encounters on her daily walk.

> Daily walk around the three mile loop
> Orange vest slipped over my parka during hunting season
> Offering the loving kindness prayer
> May all beings in these surroundings be filled with loving
>   kindness
> It's hard to acknowledge the hunters in pickup trucks
> Especially Mike, a neighbor living in the trailer with Pattie
> He had the mature spruce stand cleared
> Timbers for the house he'll someday build
> I offer loving kindness to the ravaged forest
> Think of the birds who will return in spring
> To find no conifers for nesting
> May all beings in these surroundings be happy
> Now Mike is in the back of a pick-up truck
> With two others, orange-vested and armed
> They will consider themselves fortunate
> To amplify the explosive sound of rifle discharge
> Is Mike less of a neighbor when he hunts our fellow neigh-
>   bors the deer

> May all beings in these surroundings be peaceful and at ease
> Daily walk around the three mile loop
> Orange vest slipped over my parka
> Shots in the distance
> Three men in a corn field standing over a deer
> I hope she died quickly, not like the other one
> Crossing into the woods, moving slowly, belly very bloodied
> I see the blood for days until a fresh snow falls
> May all beings in these surroundings be well and safe
> Daily walk around the three mile loop
> Orange vest slipped over my parka
> Sometimes my loving kindness prayer seems not enough or
>   simply too late
> I remember the words of one of my teachers
> "Not one drop of kindness is lost, not one drop"
> And so I continue offering phrases of loving kindness to all

In offering loving kindness to all—creatures, forests, and neighbors—Susan is practicing mature compassion. This all-inclusive caring stretches its arms to hold many perspectives. The same three-mile walk seen from Mike's perspective might show the reverence of hunting as an ancient way of life, and the spruce timbers lovingly turned into shelter for his family.

Dr. Martin Luther King was one of the most eloquent teachers of mature compassion. Here he warns us of the dangers of facile right and wrong categories: "You all know, I think, what I am trying to say—that we must try not to end up with stereotypes of those we oppose, even as they slip all of us into their stereotypes. And who are we? Let us not do to ourselves as those others do to us: try to put ourselves into one all-inclusive category—the virtuous ones as against the

evil ones, or the decent ones as against the malicious, preju-
diced ones, or the well educated as against the ignorant."

To find mature compassion we learn to skillfully walk a
tight rope—holding firm to our own truth and at the same
time flexibly respecting the truths of others. The skill of
walking this spiritual tight rope is not a wishy-washy
endeavor. It requires moral conviction, a warrior's heart, and
fierce commitment to act on what we belief. It assumes that
we'll sometimes lose our balance and fall into judgment and
righteousness. Walking the high wire of genuine compassion
demands regular spiritual practice, and a willingness to face
all the messy contradictions and inconsistencies within ourselves and the world.

This isn't easy. And it's in the heat of our discomfort
where we grow. In our relationships, our families, and our
communities we are constantly challenged to expand our caring to those who think and live differently than ourselves.
These challenges are the fertile territory of spiritual growth:
the place where the heart comes into full blossom. To follow
the full cycle of young, idealistic compassion into the ripe
phase of mature caring we return to Gary's story.

We remember in chapter thirteen Gary received a mandate from the northern forest, "Learn respect for me and you
will learn respect for yourself. Pick the trash out of my heart
and you pick it out of your soul." In response to this Gary
began picking up the trash in his community as his service
project. This excerpt from his journal summarizes his learning after several years.

For over a thousand days I have collected trash as part of my service
project. With gloves and trash bags I walk in measured stride to
remove the litter in different areas of my community, my neighborhood,

and my backyard. For as long as I can remember, I have been disquieted by visions of a world overrun by trash. Dead birds trapped and drowned by six-pack o-rings. Turtles dead or dying from ingesting carelessly dropped plastic bags, or balloons lost to the sea. Baby birds unable to eat the rubber bands their parents pick up near the mailboxes all across America. This is where my heart breaks.

When I began picking up trash it was disgusting and a burden. I ran about frantically collecting all the litter and soon I was overwhelmed by the immensity of the waste. I have struggled so hard with the hopelessness and enormity of cleaning up the trash in my community. I have felt joy in watching others pick up trash and found bliss in litter-free natural areas. But my truth now lies somewhere in between. It's been a long journey from anger, resentment, and desperate demands to a place of greater acceptance and peace. My maturing spiritual practice has helped me just "sit" with trash, aware it is there, but not overwhelmed.

These days I rise each morning and do what I can, teaching others by my simple example. I cannot make others stop leaving litter. I walk the streets of my community and know that there will always be more trash, more ecological suffering. I am beginning to understand that to really make a permanent difference I need to educate others about how to end the suffering caused by trash. The Dalai Lama said it best, "tend toward compassion." So I move with compassion toward myself, toward others, toward the earth. With gloves and bag, bending wordlessly I say a prayer of loving kindness for the earth, for the trash, and for those who left it.

Gary's story is a striking example of the journey most of us go through to reach mature compassion. He takes us back through the labyrinth of caring: starting out with glowing idealism; moving through the shadows of arrogance, overwhelm, and anger; and finally coming to a place of greater peace where he realizes he cannot fix or end the suffering caused by trash but he can respond with an open heart and presence. Once again it is spiritual practice that helps Gary embrace the paradox of acceptance and active engagement.

As he picked up the garbage left by others we watched Gary experience rage, resentment, and despair. He couldn't skip these feelings, he had to go through them in order to reach the stage where he could genuinely say, "So I move with compassion toward myself, toward others, toward the earth. With gloves and bag, bending wordlessly I say a prayer of loving kindness for the earth, for the trash, and for those who left it." Gary's heart is in full blossom as his prayers include not just the earth, but also those who cause damage by leaving the trash.

Whether we're cleaning up toxic waste, restoring a polluted river, replanting forests, working to end racism, halt child abuse, or stop violence of any kind—we'll probably go through a cycle that includes most of the feelings Gary experienced. It's important to have the support of friends, colleagues, or counselors during these times; to return to the stillness of spiritual practice to balance inner and outer; and to remember that our moments of despair are as much part of compassion as our idealism. And it's helpful to carry Dr. King's words in our hearts, "we must try not to end up with stereotypes of those we oppose."

Exercise: The Heart in Full Blossom

Using your chosen practice take about fifteen minutes to quiet your mind and open your heart. Find a peaceful place within yourself. For a few moments go back to a time in your personal story where you have already practiced this mature compassion that embraces contradictions—when you forgave your parents, confronted the wake-up call in your story, or healed your central image. Remember at those times your heart understood that there were no simplistic truths.

Imagine a societal situation where someone has different values than you do. Choose a situation that's real for you, something where it's very difficult for you to feel compassion. Now keeping your heart open feel your righteousness, your judgments, and your arrogance as you encounter this situation. Keep breathing, keep your heart open. Feel your rage and resentment, feel your despair. Feel the messy contradictions in your own life. Remember in order to find genuine compassion you have to pass through these feelings. And remember we're all a beautiful mess full of untidy paradoxes. Take time to reflect, draw, and journal.

Once again return to your practice for a few minutes quieting your mind, entering the stillness. Become aware of the infinite spaciousness of your quiet mind. Notice that in this spaciousness there is room for all points of view. This infinite stillness is soft, fluid, welcoming, without the tight boundaries of right and wrong. Now place the situation you are working with in this infinite spaciousness. Just hold it there next to your own point of view. You don't have to agree with it, just gently hold it there. Try holding your own truth and at the same time softly respecting the truth of the other person. Do this for a few minutes. If feelings of rage, righteousness, or judgment return, simply notice them and let them go. Take time to feel, reflect, draw, and describe your experience.

Visualize your quiet mind as a doorway into your open heart. Imagine your heart completely open, in full blossom. Place your hands on your heart in full blossom and listen to its gentle voice. Can you hear it whisper there are no simple truths, no tidy categories of "I am right and you are wrong."

Can you hear your heart gently remind you that invisible threads connect all of us in our joy and our sorrow—no matter what values we hold? Now once again encounter the situation you are working with. Go to the place Rumi describes where your heart is in full blossom, where differences are forgotten, and "all hearts are in unison." In this place try offering compassion to your encounter. Do this in whatever way feels genuine to you. What do you feel as you offer compassion in this situation? Take time to feel, reflect, draw, and describe your experience.

This exercise is something you can practice for the rest of your life. In your relationships, family, work, and community you are constantly challenged to expand your caring to those who think and live differently than you do. This isn't easy. But remember it's in the heat of your discomfort where you grow, and where your heart comes into full blossom.

CONCLUSION: IN HARMONY WITH OUR RHYTHM OF COMPASSION

The labyrinth is thoroughly known. We have only to follow
the thread of the hero path, and where we had thought to
find an abomination, we shall find a god. And where we had
thought to slay another, we shall slay ourselves. Where we
had thought to travel outward, we will come to the center of
our own existence. And where we had thought to be alone,
we will be with all the world.

—*Joseph Campbell, from* The Power of Myth

At some primal level each of us knows that our fundamental
well being is inseparable from the well being of the world. In
our heart of hearts we recognize that if we isolate ourselves
and disconnect from the suffering of society and the earth,
we are actually disconnecting from ourselves. We know that
this fragmentation leaves us empty, like hungry ghosts never
satisfied. The search to connect our own story to the larger
story of the world is a search for wholeness. This quest for
wholeness expresses itself in two fundamental and inseparable yearnings—self-reflection and contribution, the in-breath
and the out-breath.

In digging for the stories of self, society, and the earth we have seen that the in-breath of self-reflection gives us the clarity of heart and mind required to face our complex human and ecological challenges. Breathing in also leads to the self-care necessary to sustain our engagement with the world's suffering. We learned that when we cared for ourselves there came a time of natural ripeness when we wanted to offer our contribution to our communities. This out-breath came from a spontaneous and joyful generosity rather than moral obligation. Reaching out to the world in this way gave us rich soul nourishment. Thus we realized that soul and society are sacred partners who need each other in order to fulfill themselves.

Though we recognized them as partners, we quickly confronted the inherent challenges in the marriage between soul and society. Like any marriage, skillfully balancing the needs of our soul with the needs of the world has no clearly marked path. So we bushwhacked our way, learning to become skillful in following our rhythm—knowing when to go inward and when to go out into the community. Ultimately we each have to forge our own unique path of balancing inner and outer. Yet we discovered certain things that can support all of us. As we come home to our rhythm of compassion, this conclusion will underscore those things that help us follow our rhythm, and discuss how to sustain the balance between self-care and contribution to the world.

THE LIGHT AND SHADOW OF INNER AND OUTER

An essential key to following our rhythm of compassion is the awareness that both the inner life of self-reflection and the outer life of contribution have positive and negative attributes.

Much of our balancing capacity comes from skillfully navigating the light and shadow of both the in-breath and the out-breath. When we find ourselves in the shadow territory we're probably out of balance in some way. And when we can stay in the territory where we're nourished by the inherent gifts of either the inner or the outer, we've found our rhythm.

Digging for our personal stories illuminates many of the positive aspects of self-reflection. We uncovered what ancient alchemists called the *prima materia* that makes up our unconscious: layers of artifacts including central images, masks, parents, broken hearts, and radical surprises. Telling our story truthfully—with all its joys and sorrows—was the alchemy that transformed the separate pieces into a conscious whole. Knowing our story helped us know ourselves, a prerequisite to conscious caring. As our stories unfolded, and our self-understanding matured, we came to appreciate the positive nature of the in-breath of self-care: time to think, dream, reflect, clear out, reprioritize, pray, write poetry, and nurture the spiritual values that sustain us and allow us to move skillfully into the world.

In the deeper layers of self-reflection we learned to have compassion for our suffering—shadows, wounds, inconsistencies, and brokenness. We realized our brokenness connected us to the unbroken whole, and we were inspired to bring our compassion to others. The in-breath of self-reflection was starting to move out as we offered the lessons from our personal story to the larger story of the human family and the earth. Thus we recognized that at its most illuminated our inner search is not removed from the world, rather it propels out to our communities.

But on the other side of this light the in-breath reveals its shadow of narcissism and endless self-absorption. Here is our culture's fatigue with analysis, our obsession with dysfunction. The shadow of self-reflection might show itself in these archetypes: the person who after ten years in therapy is still trying to forgive her parents; the friend of many years who continues to be self-absorbed with his own personal healing journey, seduced into the quagmire of narcissism; the person who knows too much about the psycho-babble of dysfunction and almost nothing about her local community and environmental programs; the colleague who believes he has to totally get himself together before he can contribute to society; the therapist who feels burned out on personal problems and needs to move out into the collective.

In these shadowy archetypes we see the in-breath imploding upon itself and leading to the dead end of spiritual emptiness. Here the vital medicine is not more self-reflection, but the out-breath of passionate engagement with the world.

As we become more whole we yearn for a place to channel our moral energy. Bernie Glassman, abbot of the Zen community in New York City, described the transition from the in-breath of self-awareness to the out-breath of engagement when he said, "If you were to ask me 'what is the essence of Buddhism?' I would answer that it's to awaken. And that the function of that awakening is learning how to serve." Our inner awakening comes into full blossom as we contribute to society and the earth. And with the life of contribution we learn that it is crucial to expose the shadow of our motivation if we are to serve with genuine compassion.

Confronting our social and ecological shadow we entered a maze of intense and conflicting impulses. We wanted to fix, control, be the expert, or play God in order to get society or the earth the way we thought it should be. We were startled to find our need for approval, status, and power; feelings of shame, do-goodism, should, perfectionism, and looking better than others—all mixed up with the genuine desire to care. Sometimes we became righteous about our social or ecological causes, falling into the trap of my way is right and the others are wrong. After a lot of digging we found that what gave all these shadows their potency was the insidious illusion that we are different or separate from those we serve, or those who have different values than we do.

Just like the in-breath has its shadowy archetypes so does the out-breath: the dedicated activist who uses her cause as a defense for never looking inward; the service workaholic whose addiction to service leads to burn out and compassion fatigue; the person whose contribution is fueled by guilt and compulsive do-goodism rather than authentic caring; the politically correct friend who is always reminding you how great he is and how unevolved you are; the colleague who looks like she's dedicated to environmental change but on the inside is deeply cynical, convinced it's too late to repair the damage.

We learned to put aside our embarrassment and expose our shadows to the light of self-awareness, talking with colleagues or getting help from mentors, counselors, or support groups. With appropriate respect for the dark side of service, we could move into the rich and sometimes unexpected gifts of contributing to the world. The most obvious reward, and perhaps the most precious, was the realization that entering the heart of human and ecological suffering caused momentary pain, but gave us lasting fulfillment.

We learned to open to the suffering, to feel it, to connect with it, and to let it flow through us. As we engaged with the pain rather than running away from it, we healed our alienation from each other and the natural world. We recognized that separation and alienation were the deeper roots of our pain, not just the societal or environmental problems themselves. Now we were seeing the true nature of suffering and learning to respond to it skillfully. This insight into the world's suffering put our own pain into proper perspective and we could see how our story fit into the larger scheme of the human family and planetary story.

An unexpected gift of service and stewardship was that it compelled us to find out what really mattered. To make a contribution to our communities many of us had to reprioritize our lives, clearing away incessant busyness and the multitude of things that drained our energy. To care for the earth we were asked to create sustainable lifestyles that lead to simpler, cleaner living. We discovered that living in an earth-friendly way helped break our collective addiction to the consumerism that left us with hollow lives.

Consuming less and contributing more nourished our souls with the rewards of beauty, peace of mind, family, community, and time for the almost lost pleasures of real conversation, walking, and reading. Generosity of spirit allows us not only to be our brother, sister, and earth's keeper, but guardian of our own spirit. And the circle returned, as the out-breath of caring for the world lead back to rich inner fulfillment.

THE FRIENDS OF BALANCE

Our task now is not to fix the blame for the past, but to fix the course for the future.

—*President John F. Kennedy*

Along with carefully navigating the light and shadow of inner and outer, there are certain qualities that help us balance caring for self and society. We learned to respect these friends of balance as lifelong practices, not glib prescriptions that pretend finding our rhythm is quick or easy.

The greatest friend of all is our chosen spiritual practice. We realized that we each find the practice, or combination of practices, that works best for us. Regardless of the form, our practice is a time for silence and solitude. It is a time to reconnect with our spirit, quiet our mind, and open our heart. Whether we sit on a meditation cushion, kneel in prayer, breathe with a yoga posture, or find sacred time in nature— our practice is the quiet space from which we listen to our rhythm.

In the stillness of our practice we can hear our rhythm of compassion breath in and out: it's time to rest I've done enough; I feel my heart call to help the teenagers, or protect the whales, or sit with the dying; I am getting righteous, there are many different ways to see the issue I'm working on; busyness is eating me up, I need to stop, take a retreat, be good to myself; in prayer this morning I feel guided to volunteer with battered women. In this quiet time devoted to spiritual practice we hear how to care for ourselves and our communities.

If we devote ourselves to our chosen practice, spending time each day or at least several times a week, we begin to experience the subtler rewards of practice. We notice the stillness softens the edges of our ego helping us let go of the need to fix, control, or run away from suffering. The open heart cultivated through dedicated practice is able to hold complex contradictions breaking the rigid ego boundaries of right and wrong, either, or. The beauty of any mature practice is that it naturally balances the inner and outer. It knows that reflection and engagement are the two halves of a fully lived life.

Along with the great friend of spiritual practice we explored imagination, discipline, and support as qualities that help us skillfully follow our rhythm of compassion. Imagination reminds us that finding our rhythm is a creative process more than anything else. We experiment with different kinds of self-renewal, discovering what most fully nourishes us and how often we need the in-breath. David and I have found we need the healing of the ocean and we take several seaside retreats every year. Sometimes our imagination guides us to a weekend of hiking, a day of solitude and silence, time to share deeply with beloved friends, an evening of poetry, music, or theater as ways to restore ourselves. We have found that even a small dose of creative in-breath goes a long way in refreshing and restoring us.

Imagination needs the friends of discipline and support in order to ground its creative impulses. Our busy lives require a disciplined hand to clear away space for what matters to us—be it self-care or caring for the world. For most of us juggling inner and outer simply isn't going to happen without a certain amount of vigilant planning and priority setting. In this context, discipline is taking a stand for quality of life for our communities and us.

Over and over again the stories we've heard teach us that the role of support is crucial in staying with our rhythm of compassion. This support can come through friends, family, and community, as well as professional help from counselors and mentors. The fundamental truth at the heart of support is that we can't grow alone. We need reflection in order to see ourselves in both our beauty and distortion.

Support is what fuels compassion: the therapist who helps you uncover and heal the shadow of your core wound so you don't project it onto the people you serve; a mentor who supports you in overcoming your fear of suffering and your false need to fix it; the spiritual director who guides you toward a spiritual practice and then helps you stay committed to it; the men's group who tells you when you're burned out or self-righteous and in need of self-renewal; and the friend or family member who knows you well enough to point out your self-absorption and suggest you move outward and contribute to the community. Without support the already difficult challenge of balancing soul and society becomes almost impossible. You don't have to do it alone. There is a multitude of possibilities just waiting to support, reflect, and nourish you.

THE SUSTAINERS: BELONGING, BELIEVING, AND TRUSTING

There is nobody on the planet, neither those whom we see as the oppressed nor those whom we see as the oppressor, who doesn't have what it takes to wake up. . . . The source of all wakefulness, the source of all kindness and compassion, the source of all wisdom, is in each second of time.

—*Pema Chodron, from* When Things Fall Apart

Along with the friends of balance there is a trinity of inner qualities that are crucial in sustaining our rhythm of compassion. Belonging, believing, and trusting are the fruits of spiritual practice, imagination, discipline, and support. This trinity helps sustain the balance between inner and outer throughout the inevitable challenges of life.

We have discussed the importance of belonging to your place, putting down deep roots in your home landscape—be it urban or rural. We have seen how belonging is the natural witness to the inner and outer cycles of your life, holding both with equal honor and tenderness. When you live in harmony with the seasons and cycles of your place, it teaches you to do the same within yourself. In this way belonging to a place provides the grounding for your rhythm. You return to the refuge of your place to attune to your rhythm, listening for when to go in and when to go out. The roots of belonging to your place are bound together with the roots of belonging to yourself and your community. This interwoven belonging helps us sustain our caring for soul and society.

Another sustainer of compassion is believing that we make a difference. This is not a light-weight believing. Rather it is a faith forged in the fire of heartbreak, looking the immensity of the world's suffering straight in the eyes. This believing that we make a difference is built on moral conviction, nitty-gritty pragmatism, and dedication to the inner life. It understands that our response to the world is a configuration of our moral beliefs, a mirror not only to what we believe about society, but also ourselves.

This kind of belief is the spiritual muscle of compassion, giving us strength when the going gets tough, and lifting us out of the inevitable moments of despair. This belief constitutes an abiding faith in Pema Chodron's powerful words "There is nobody on the planet, neither those whom we see as the oppressed nor those whom we see as the oppressor, who doesn't have what it takes to wake up."

In our cynical and jaded times it's not always easy to maintain this belief. Sometimes when I hear the never ending, numbing, negative news reports I doubt that anything I do can help our world. In those moments I have learned to call forth an image. I imagine all the hands I know on deck: I see Diane changing the way we treat people with AIDS; Sonya is revisioning early childhood education; Supe is working to end racism; Pat is humanizing the prison system; David is teaching the pleasures of simple sustainable living; Ann is educating us how to care for the creatures; Jeff is protecting the wetlands; and Teresa is giving respect and dignity to those who are dying. I add my hands to theirs and realize how many of us are doing what the theologian Thomas Berry calls "the great work." None of us can do everything, but we can each do our part of the great work, knowing that all together we make the difference in creating the world we all hope for.

The final quality in the trinity of sustainers is trusting. We have seen that the process of balancing inner and outer is highly individual, changing with the different cycles of our lives. Learning to trust these larger cycles is key to maintaining our rhythm. Some of us find our rhythm balancing both the in-breath and the out-breath simultaneously, while others tend to concentrate on one or the other during different cycles of life.

As a way to cultivate trust I asked my students to examine their rhythm of compassion throughout the cycles of their lives. In this journal entry, Anne describes her growing trust. Anne is an inspiring yoga teacher and a vibrant, ageless grandmother.

> I live my life in growing orbits
> that move out over the world.
> perhaps I can never achieve the last,
> but that will be my attempt.
> I am circling around God, around the ancient tower,
> and I have been circling for a thousand years,
> and I still don't know if I am a falcon, or a storm,
> or a great song.
>
> —*Rainer Maria Rilke*

The falcon, the storm, and the great song express the varied in-breath and out-breath times in my life. Without conscious planning my life has followed a pattern, a normal rhythm of in and out, that goes along with my life transitions.

Early childhood, lots of in-breath. Entering college I felt a freedom to finally breathe out engaging with the world. My twenties, child bearing, and child rearing kept the focus on my family. Motherhood was a meaningful in-breath. Quiet, focused, I was the falcon.

Then come my thirties and forties where I balance both the in-breath and the out-breath. The storm begins with a marital affair that was pivotal in changing my life. Rapid personal growth and introspection along with strong community leadership. Every summer the conscious in-breath of retreat: packed kids, dog, bathing suits, books, and scrabble game and turned inward for two months of ocean healing. The storm blows harder with the death of my father, my family's commitment to twelve-step work to learn about our addiction, and a rigorous examination of my marriage in attempts to keep it alive.

My fifties: divorce, aftermath of the storm. I go deeply inward, no community leadership. I fight for my very survival creating a new life for myself, by myself.

My sixties: finally I find I can live like a song. I give voice to my life experiences, I honor my creative powers. I am able to balance community participation and self-care. I have found my great song, I have found my rhythm. Still I am circling the ancient tower.

Anne's lovely statement—"Without conscious planning my life has followed a pattern, a natural rhythm of in and out that goes along with my life transitions"—has much to teach us. We see that sometimes she balanced both the inner life and community leadership, and at other times she needed to go just into herself to heal. Like Maud's story, Anne's trust came with the wisdom of a fully lived life—honestly facing the joys and sorrows within herself and the world. Anne's story illuminates that our rhythm is inherent, already inside us just waiting for us to listen and trust. This rhythm is circular, organically flowing from inner to outer, part of a fuller cycle than either one alone. Indeed it is trust that initiates us into the seamless unity between inner and outer.

IN HARMONY WITH OUR RHYTHM

Over time as we take heed of light and shadow, cultivate our spiritual practice, and stay close to the friends of balance and sustainers of compassion—we gradually become skillful in following our rhythm of compassion. Following our rhythm gives us an inner cadence of contentment as we balance the expectations from our family and our contribution to the world with our own self-renewal and spiritual growth.

As we live more and more within our rhythm, the inner and the outer become indistinguishable. The waves and the ocean are one.

Now there is no longer so much inner and outer as there is a continuous reflection back and forth. In this two-way mirror we recognize that what we have compassion for inside ourselves, we can have compassion for out in the world. What we reject out in society and the earth is what we reject within ourselves. As we learn to have compassion for our own wounds, shadows, and inconsistencies we also are more capable of loving that in others. Conversely, as we learn compassion for the underbelly, judgments, or righteousness out in the world, we are more able to forgive that in ourselves. In this excerpt from Chris's journal, she portrays this seamless rhythm between inner and outer by using the symbol of a boomerang.

THE BOOMERANG OF COMPASSION

The boomerang: We send it out. It returns. We send it out again. It returns again and again.

So with my rhythm of compassion.

The call to serve comes from within, from that vibrating, inner resonance, that chord that is struck when seeing pain, need, helplessness, opportunity. I find compassion.

I take the boomerang into my hand.

The energy for the service also comes from within. From the reverberations of the chord come the motivation, the energy, and the nourishment to continue to serve—and find compassion.

I launch the boomerang.

The outer service raises inner conflicts, inner fears, inner questions. I find myself reflected in those I serve. I ask the question: Where does one end and the other begin? —and find compassion.

The boomerang returns, as a mirror. To continue to serve, I must look in the mirror and acknowledge light and dark—and find compassion.

The circle goes on.

One conflict, one fear, one question is resolved. With renewed inner energy, I launch the boomerang once more, and my arm has been strengthened.

And once again, it returns to raise another fear, another conflict, another squirming I-don't-want-to-face-this-truth. Look in the mirror, see my complicity—and find compassion.

Sometimes it's too hard, too terrifying, too close to face what I learn. I put the boomerang away—often without compassion.

But compassion is the spring rain that washes, reawakens, and rekindles the heart. It can once again rejuvenate the arm to retrieve the boomerang and launch it once again.

In Chris's lovely words we can feel the eternal rhythm of compassion. She shows us that this rhythm is made up of the counterpoint between the inner and outer, and if we don't have both there is no rhythm. And Chris helps us see that when self-reflection and engagement with the world are in tune, we experience a harmonious flow where the notes of inner and outer unite as one. In a moment of absolute stillness during meditation, we feel as if we're actively encountering the suffering of the world. Or in a moment of intense engaged caring for someone, we feel utterly still as if we are praying.

Although we might have thought of the inner and the outer as living in separate houses, we find they are more like different rooms under the same roof. Each offers space for unique aspects of the self to develop, but both provide the shelter of meaning and wholeness. In this excerpt from George's journal we see the reflection between inner and outer, and how each contributes to George's sense of meaning. In earlier chapters you met George, a high-level computer consultant, who was searching for his arena of service. He found his path of service in the "Alternatives to Violence Program" in the Colorado State Prisons where he has been a trainer for the last several years.

A few months ago, I experienced my first visit to a women's prison. I had gone with great curiosity about how it would feel relative to my work in the men's prison. Unsurprisingly, it was chattier, noisier, and friendlier—in a way.

But I was shocked to find out that almost all the women were mothers. Young mothers. One of the women, an attractive, energetic young girl/woman/mother had a husband who was also in prison. She herself had grown up in an abusive family where her parents were criminals. What, I thought, would become of her children?

As always in my prison visits I felt very close, and in a psychological way, very similar to these fellow beings who had somehow taken paths so different than mine. In the film "Shawshank Redemption" a prisoner gets paroled after fifty years behind walls. Outside, he is unable to cope and hangs himself. When they hear about his death, his fellows back in prison understand. He has been "institutionalized" they say.

I too have been institutionalized. Walled up in my mind. A mental object, a boxed-up compendium of a certain height and weight with describable accomplishments, relationships, and activities. Unaware of feeling—disconnected—no in-breath, no out-breath. Holding my breath.

Can my imprisoned friends be rehabilitated after being institutionalized? I hope so. I think this has to happen by breaking patterns. By being put into new surroundings and given care, understanding, and love. That's what helped me, maybe it can help them too.

I am proud to say that I now give myself permission to be still. I now give myself permission to feel, and to be out of my mind. I have begun the in-breath. And I have begun the out-breath. Beginning as a service assignment, it has progressed from soup kitchens to prisons, and now has become part of my life.

Where all this leads, I don't know. But I think it is leading to a place inside me where I am at home. To the house of God, where God's glory abides.

To find our rhythm is, indeed, to come home to ourselves. To find a state of harmony where we fully inhabit our inner lives, as well as fully engage in the life of society and the earth. We are at home both inside and outside. Both in the small intimate house of our own belonging, as well as belonging to the immensity of the house of the world. Perhaps we cannot really belong unless we belong to both.

Seven years ago I intuitively entitled the training this book is based upon, "Grace." It's only now that I understand the fuller significance of the word I chose. When we find our rhythm of compassion we have come home, we are in a state of grace. We are in tune with a great universal cadence where a rich inner life is exquisitely balanced with a passionate engagement with the world. Conversely we need grace—"an unmerited gift from God"—to find that universal rhythm.

My role as a teacher becomes more and more simple, to midwife the discovery of this natural grace. To encourage those I work with to listen to their rhythm and trust the natural ebb and flow of their cycles. To remind them that intrinsic to this state of grace is a spirit of compassion that gives moral standing to all living things.

This book connects that spirit of compassion to the lived experience—people's stories. These stories have shown human nature at its most generous. They have demonstrated our complex and inexplicable caring for each other, and for our life together here on this earth. I believe they have also demonstrated a simultaneous yearning for personal awakening along with a profound concern for others: an understanding that the revolution of caring must occur both within and without.

These stories have also illuminated the moral passion of those who have made inspiring commitments to changing both psyche and the world. They are an invitation to find that moral energy within yourself, be it motivated by religious, political, or humanistic values. This moral passion will guide you to respond to the complex times we live in with reflection and responsibility. It will help you examine yourself and find out what you really value; open your heart to society's suffering and offer generous compassion; and listen to the voices of the earth and hear the call of humane stewardship.

Perhaps there is no stronger call today than to use our growing consciousness to wisely shape a future that is both soulful and sustainable. The Italian poet and educator, Danilo

Dolce, inspired President Kennedy to create the Peace Corps when he wrote, "We must tend to all three levels—self, society, and the earth—if we wish to make any lasting and beneficial changes." We do this not only because it makes the world a better place, but because these revolutionary acts of caring are also where our deepest joy resides.

ACKNOWLEDGMENTS

To Ned Leavitt, agent extraordinaire, warrior, brother, and dear friend whose belief in this book allowed me to believe in it. Deepest appreciation to Ned for his astute shaping of the manuscript and finding a home for it at Tuttle. To my editor, Jan Johnson for her keen vision of this book's potential and brilliant, kind, and humorous guidance. To Caroline Pincus for her editorial support and the experience of genuine collaboration. I am forever grateful to Valerie Andrews for her superb mentoring and for teaching me how to write. To my beloved friend, Ellen Wingard for reading early versions and giving me the confidence I needed. To Robyn Heisey at Tuttle for her support and for graciously answering every question I asked. To Martha Hill for her impeccable transcriptions of my students' journal entries.

To my *Grace* students without whom this book would never have been written. Thank you for sharing your lives and teaching me. Thank you for having the courage to enter the fierce fires of suffering—your own and the world's—so that we could all deepen in compassion together. To all of you—those whose stories are included in this book as well as those who offered their stories—I salute you and I love you.

To Bert Shaw, consummate spiritual mentor, for guiding me through my healing journey with such skill and compassion—so that I could learn to do the same for others. To Moira Shaw for her genius and generosity in making the Pathwork Lectures vibrant and accessible to all of us. To the Pathwork Lectures themselves for being my chosen spiritual text and for continuing to change my life and the lives of so many of my students.

To my community in Woodstock, New York, whose love and support has blessed my life beyond measure. Abundant gratitude to Joseph Jastrab, Bert and Moira Shaw, Jeanne Nametz, Ned Leavitt and Lynn Margileth, Elizabeth Lesser and Tom Bullard, Kali Rosenblum and Kevin Smith, George and Helen Kaufman, Judith Garten, Phyllis Luberg, Elizabeth Rose Campbell, Linda Kauer, Joanie Zinter, and special thanks in memory of Peter Hendrickson and Tim Allen. To my Helix sisters—Ellen Wingard, Guinilla Norris, Danit Fried, and Ro King—for nineteen years, and going strong, of the richest, most outrageous sisterhood. To my sister, Joanie Mclean for the deepening of our sisterhood as we grow older together.

To the Grandmother Mountains near my home for guiding me with their profound and constant presence. And finally to my husband, David Gershon for his unfaltering support, inspiration, and kindness—for being the love of my life—and for being the embodiment of the principles of this book.

For Further Support

For further information on the Grace Spiritual Growth Training Program this book is based upon, as well as information on Empowerment Workshops, books, and audio cassettes contact:

Empowerment Training Programs
1649 Rt. 28A
West Hurley, New York 12491
Fax: 914-331-3041
E-mail: gstraub@empowermenttraining.com
Web Site: www.empowermenttraining.com

For further information on Global Action Plan's sustainable living programs for households, neighborhoods, and children contact:

Global Action Plan
P.O. Box 428
Woodstock, New York 12498
Tel: 914-679-4830
Fax: 914- 679-4834
E-mail: info@globalactionplan.org
Web Site: www.globalaction.org